# Understanding enduring ideas in education: A response to those who 'just want to be a teacher'

# Understanding enduring ideas in education: A response to those who 'just want to be a teacher'

*Edited by*
Carol Mutch and Jennifer Tatebe

NZCER PRESS
New Zealand Council for Educational Research
PO Box 3237
Wellington
New Zealand

www.nzcer.org.nz

© Authors 2017

ISBN 978-1-98-854208-9

No part of the publication may be copied, stored, or communicated in any form by any means (paper or digital), including recording or storing in an electronic retrieval system, without the written permission of the publisher.
Education institutions that hold a current licence with Copyright Licensing New Zealand may copy from this book in strict accordance with the terms of the CLNZ Licence.

A catalogue record for this book is available from the National Library of New Zealand.

Designed by Smartwork Creative Ltd, www.smartworkcreative.co.nz

# Contents

| | |
|---|---|
| Preface | 1 |
| Glossary | 5 |
| Chapter 1 Introduction: Becoming teachers and the value of philosophical thinking<br>Claudia Rozas Gómez | 9 |
| Discussion starters | 26 |

*Tradition 1: Progressivism*

| | |
|---|---|
| Progressivism—a personal reflection<br>Peter O'Connor | 27 |
| Progressivism—history and concepts<br>Chapter 2 Understanding progressive education and its influence on policy and pedagogy in New Zealand<br>Carol Mutch | 31 |
| Thinking about progressivism in today's world<br>Chapter 3 Weaving our whāriki: Re-imagining progressive philosophy in Aotearoa New Zealand early childhood education<br>Jacoba Matapo and John Roder | 47 |
| Discussion starters | 62 |

*Tradition 2: Liberalism*

| | |
|---|---|
| Liberalism—a personal reflection<br>Maria Perreau | 63 |
| Liberalism—history and concepts<br>Chapter 4 Daring to know: The liberal tradition and education<br>Alexis Siteine | 67 |
| Thinking about liberalism and progressivism in today's world<br>Chapter 5 Rethinking what it means to be a teacher through a mixed modality approach<br>Graham McPhail | 82 |

Discussion starters ......... 95

*Tradition 3: Socially critical perspectives*

Socially critical perspectives—a personal reflection ......... 97
Fetaui Iosefo

Socially critical perspectives—history and concepts
    Chapter 6  Critical awakening: Teaching and learning a politicised world ......... 103
Jennifer Tatebe

Thinking about socially critical perspectives in today's world
    Chapter 7  Kaupapa Māori: Decolonising politics and philosophy in education ......... 119
Mera Lee-Penehira

Discussion starters ......... 136

Index ......... 137

# Preface

The adage "those who can, do; those who can't, teach" could not be further from the truth. This adaptation of George Bernard Shaw's line from the play *Man and Superman* is an enduring trope that the authors of the various contributions to this book insightfully dismantle. Instead, this book responds by presenting the process of becoming a teacher as a site of contested and often competing ideas. A well-known tension faced by teacher–educators is the divide students see between theory and practice. Preservice teachers often struggle to understand the rationale behind learning about theory, philosophy, and politics—or the "big ideas" of education. In the early stages of their development, they can have a narrow conception of what really matters on their journey to becoming teachers.

We recognise that the visible and tangible learning that occurs in classrooms and schools on practicum placements is an integral aspect of teacher preparation. This book, however, makes a strong argument for the importance of deep thinking about the nature and purpose of the career preservice teachers are embarking upon. A common activity in teacher preparation programmes is for preservice teachers to articulate their personal philosophy of teaching: What kind of teacher do they want to become? What aspects of teaching and learning are most important to them? It is important for them to understand that none of the beliefs that teachers have or the choices that they make exist in a vacuum. All these ideas have come from somewhere—often far back in history—and have been challenged and debated over many decades as scholars have attempted to resolve the big questions of education and schooling.

So, what are the big questions of education? In the first chapter of this book, Claudia Rozas Gómez suggests what some of these might be:

1. What are the aims of education?
2. What is teaching?
3. What does the educated person look like?
4. What is the best knowledge to teach?
5. What kind of a society do we want to live in?
6. What kind of people do we want to be?
7. How might education enable these ideals?

In this book, we address these and other questions from different standpoints and discuss how the responses to such questions have left enduring legacies. In doing so, we also model how educational ideas are political and contested. A key challenge is how to make the relationship between educational philosophy, politics, and theory relevant to teachers' practice. By drawing on local, national, and global research, and personal professional expertise, we aim to support future teachers to understand and explore the theoretical, philosophical, and political origins of their own views of education.

All the authors in this edited collection have taught politics and philosophy of education courses at the University of Auckland's Faculty of Education and Social Work. Similarly, all authors are educators with experience of teaching in a range of early childhood, primary, secondary, and tertiary settings in Aotearoa New Zealand and abroad. The appeal of the book will be much wider than our specific teacher education courses, however, as these are ideas also discussed in other undergraduate and postgraduate courses in education, philosophy, policy, and sociology.

The idea for this book came in response to recurring themes in student feedback over several years. Our preservice teachers find the compulsory politics and philosophy undergraduate course to be one of the most challenging in their teaching preparation. For many, this is the first engagement with educational politics and philosophy; they are expecting a "how to" course that will give them comforting answers to the ethical, philosophical, and political dilemmas they might face. Instead, we challenge their assumptions, systematically pull apart their taken-for-granted beliefs, and meet their questions with more questions. Not only is the content of the course a challenge to some, many find the assigned readings for the course difficult, even inaccessible. By putting the course content in one place, with chapters written by people who know the course well, we hope that our beginning teachers will find their way through the maze of ideas in a more logical and coherent manner.

There are many different ways that we could have approached this book, but we chose to draw on Dean's (2014) idea of a "thought collective", where individuals recognise and discuss connecting concepts within a common framework. If we took three such thought collectives and examined them in more depth, this would avoid overwhelming our students and over-trivialising important ideas. It would also allow us to explore the contested nature of such ideas. Dean suggests that a thought collective approach "allows for a multiplicity of viewpoints and different national and transnational developments, borrowings and mutations" (p. 151). We chose to focus on three thought collectives, or philosophical traditions, that impact on education policy and practice today—progressive, liberal, and socially critical perspectives. The book centres on these three enduring lenses through which many educators and scholars have sought answers to the big questions of education.

The book begins with Claudia Rozas Gómez setting a framework for examining the big questions of education and approaching teaching as a *thinking life*. She suggests an approach based on *asking*, *examining*, and *becoming*. Far from this chapter being abstract and esoteric, Gómez uses the ideas from some of the writers she introduces to engage in several of today's pressing debates: What would Dewey say about charter schools? What would Freire say about shifting preservice teacher education from universities and into schools? How might we respond to National Standards and high-stakes testing from a liberal knowledge perspective?

From there, the book is divided into three sections—progressive, liberal, and socially critical. Each section begins with a reflective piece where an experienced educator discusses what one of the chosen three traditions means to them, how it has influenced their lives, and how it resonates with today's issues. These vignettes are designed to place the tradition's key ideas in context before the underpinning ideas are explored in more depth.

The reflective pieces are followed by an exploration of each tradition written by an academic with expertise in that topic. How and where did this tradition originate? What are the key concepts in this tradition? What are the debates within this tradition? How has the tradition been shaped over time? What are the critiques of this tradition?

The third contribution to each section takes an aspect of that tradition and discusses it more critically to highlight the contested nature of ideas within and between these thought collectives. The three parts of each section introduce and reinforce key concepts within the tradition, yet reflect the book's approach: that there are no easy answers to these big questions, only ideas to be explored, positions to be debated, and more questions to be asked. Each section concludes with discussion suggestions that could be used to engage with the ideas introduced within and across the three traditions.

In conclusion, this book offers a way of making sense of big ideas for which there are often no concrete answers. By presenting different philosophical traditions as thought collectives, we offer multiple ways of navigating contrasting perspectives on education, while also offering the possibility of embracing elements of a variety of philosophical views. The authors of the contributions to this book illustrate that politics and philosophy can help us to understand how ideas and beliefs about education directly influence the practices of teaching and learning today. In this way, preservice teachers and other students of educational theory, philosophy, and politics can place their own emerging philosophies of education within a wider context and reflect on what drew them to education as an area of study, a topic of research, or a life-long career.

Finally, we would like to thanks all those who made this book possible: the many students who have passed through our courses and challenged our thinking; the many academics who have taught on these courses since their inception and passed their ideas onto us; the many writers and theorists whose work we never tire of reading; the individual contributors to this edited collection; the School of Critical Studies in Education for financial and moral support; and David Ellis and the staff at NZCER Press for helping our plans come to fruition.

Carol Mutch
Jennifer Tatebe

*School of Critical Studies in Education*
*Faculty of Education and Social Work*
*The University of Auckland*

## *References*

Dean, M. (2014). Rethinking neoliberalism. *Journal of Sociology*, 50, 150–163. doi:10.1177/1440783312442256

Shaw, G.B. (1903). *Man and superman*. Cambridge, MA: The University Press.

# Glossary

## *General*

**critical theory**—a philosophical approach to holding society and the status quo up to critique

**culture**—the recognisable social features and behaviours that define a group or society

**curriculum**—the outline of what a schooling system is expected to pass on to the next generation

**early childhood education (ECE)**—education for children from 0–8 years

**education**—a system of organising and implementing the passing on of knowledge and skills

**ideology**—a strongly held mindset that is seen as taken-for-granted and not open to critique

**initial teacher education (ITE)**—a common expression for teacher preparation programmes

**liberalism**—a political and educational philosophy based on freedom of the individual

**neo-conservatism**—a political and education ideology that focuses on traditional values, hierarchies, and stratification

**neoliberalism**—an economic and political ideology that focuses on the market-based principles

**pedagogy**—the art of, or structured approach to, teaching

**personal teaching philosophy**—a statement of a teacher's personal beliefs and practices of teaching

**philosophy**—the study of the nature of knowledge, reality, and morality

**philosopher**—thinker or writer who poses answers to the questions of existence and ideas

**policy**—a formal statement of how and why certain matters should be conducted

**politics**—the art or strategy of choosing decision makers and making decisions

**practice**—the practical carrying out of a set of theoretical ideas

**practicum**—practice undertaken in the field or workplace, especially when learning

**practitioner**—someone who practices their craft or profession

**praxis**—acting in way that has a wider social justice purpose

**preservice teacher**—a teacher education student before they gain formal status as a teacher

**profession**—jobs that require higher level qualifications and often have an associated code of practice

**progressivism**—a philosophical tradition that focuses on educating the whole child

**socially critical perspectives**—a catch-all phrase for many of the areas of focus that come under the critical theory umbrella, such as feminism, post-colonialism, or queer theory

**schooling**—the formal context in which children and young people aged 5–18 are taught

**society**—a formal group of people with a recognisable geographical, cultural, or political affiliation, such as a nation state

**sociology**—the study of how societies, and groups within society, function

**theory**—an explanation of the relationship between key ideas

**theorist**—a thinker or writer who puts forward a theory that provides a useful explanation for a set of ideas or events

**thought collective**—when a set of ideas coalesces and is easily recognisable

**tradition**—an action that has been undertaken or a belief that has been held for a long time

**traditional**—a set of beliefs or actions that has been carried out in a particular way over time

## *Māori*

**hapū**—kinship group, clan, tribe, subtribe; section of a large kinship group and the primary political unit in traditional Māori society

**iwi**—extended kinship group, tribe, nation, people, nationality, race—often refers to a large group of people descended from a common ancestor and associated with a distinct territory

**kaupapa Māori**—Māori approach, Māori topic, Māori customary practice, Māori institution, Māori agenda, Māori principles, Māori ideology; a philosophical doctrine, incorporating the knowledge, skills, attitudes, and values of Māori society

**mauri**—life principle, vital essence, special nature, a material symbol of a life principle, source of emotions—the essential quality and vitality of a being or entity. Also, used for a physical object, individual, ecosystem or social group in which this essence is located.

**mokopuna (grandchild)**—child or grandchild of a son, daughter, nephew, niece; descendant

**te ao Māori**—the Māori world

**tikanga Māori**—culture, custom, ethic, formality, lore, manner, method, protocol, style. Generally taken to mean "the Māori way of doing things".

**tūpuna**—ancestors, grandparents

**tūrangawaewae**—domicile, standing, place where one has the right to stand—place where one has rights of residence and belonging through kinship and whakapapa

**whakapapa**—a line of descent from one's ancestors; genealogy

**whānau**—extended family, family group, a familiar term of address to a number of people— the primary economic unit of traditional Māori society. In the modern context, the term is sometimes used to include friends who may not have any kinship ties to other members.

Chapter 1
# Introduction: Becoming teachers and the value of philosophical thinking

Claudia Rozas Gómez

*School of Critical Studies in Education*
*Faculty of Education and Social Work*
*The University of Auckland*

**Abstract**

Becoming a teacher is not the same as learning to teach. Many students enter preservice teacher programmes with a view to obtaining the best methods in order to be the best teachers. When presented with sociological and philosophical frameworks, students often resist these in favour of more practical learning. In this chapter, I write that becoming a teacher requires a commitment to ideas and to a thinking life and that philosophy of education offers the opportunity to foster deep thinking. I use the verb thinking intentionally to denote the action present in philosophical spaces. As Noddings (2007) points out: philosophy is an activity; it is something that we *do*. A thinking life rests upon a deep engagement with ideas as well as the posing of meaningful questions about the aims and ideals of education. The chapter begins by exploring the notion of education as an idea and briefly outlines some key enduring ideas that shape Western education. Next, I suggest some enduring questions that enable teachers to participate in education in thoughtful and critical ways. Finally, I discuss the value of a personal teaching philosophy and why it is important to develop a philosophy encompassing more than practice and in which a broad commitment to education is inherent.

**Key words**
Initial teacher education—philosophy of education—personal teaching philosophy

## Introduction

Education is an idea we made up. True story. We don't often talk about education as an idea; its *givenness* in society means we tend to talk about it in concrete and taken-for-granted ways. One effect of this assumed, self-evident nature is that it limits opportunities to think about education in complex ways. Consequently, preservice teachers often come to initial teacher education with a desire and a demand for practical learning (Clark, 2004). However, all teaching, learning, and schooling practices are formed out of ideas. As educational philosopher Kieran Egan reminds us, we have the schools that we have "as a result of the ideas that we hold" (Egan, 2001, p. 940). Any meaningful study of teaching therefore requires us to encounter education as a construct, as an imprecise idea we invented rather than a fully formed object we discovered. At the heart of this chapter is the assertion that ideas matter and that they matter to teachers. In this vein, I write that becoming a teacher involves more than learning to teach. Instead, I suggest becoming a teacher involves developing a commitment to ideas and to thinking about them in robust ways. In the context of this chapter, this is referred to as philosophical thinking.

Ideas are worth examining because they signal a contested space in education. Our conceptions of education are not only multiple, but regularly sit in tension with each other (Egan, 2001). Consider, for example, two regularly stated aims of education: socialisation and autonomy. The first requires inculcation into accepted social norms and habits. The second requires the development of independent thought, including the ability to question and reject social norms. How does education deal with competing societal needs such as these? One answer is that education can never fully resolve these tensions; all it can really do is mediate between them. So, although we may speak about education as a coherent entity, it is in fact a fragmented realm of competing and contested ideas.

Education's nebulous nature should be compelling to teachers. It suggests that education is, in a manner of speaking, "up for grabs" and that teachers play a central role in determining the meanings they give to education in their classrooms. This is a much broader conception of teaching than one which constitutes teachers primarily as skilled practitioners. The ability to engage with ideas about the wider purposes of education indicates a particular way of being and behaving in education spaces. It affords teachers a broader professional identity, positioning them as *critical* practitioners, and as significant mediators between policy and practice. I refer here to the kind of learning Barnett (2009) calls a process of "coming-to-know" (p. 429). It is not enough, he argues, to simply acquire a set of skills or even information; being educated is about developing the dispositions required for encountering knowledge.

Philosophical thinking allows preservice teachers to encounter education in complex ways and to develop a questioning and reflective stance within education. Philosophy enables systematic inquiry with its own questions, as well as its own methods for producing and evaluating knowledge. This is not to diminish the importance of effective practice. There are better ways to teach and teachers should be committed to strengthening practice, but becoming a teacher involves more than methods and skills. This chapter, then, is not an argument against practice; rather, it is an argument for expanding our conception of what it means to be a teacher. It also resists contemporary education shifts from "knowing to doing" (Barnett, 2009, p. 430), which currently inform initial teacher education. This move toward measurable competencies is reframing teaching in particular ways, emphasising the practical over the intellectual.

Approaching education via a philosophical lens encourages preservice teachers to develop certain dispositions that change who they become as teachers in profound and substantial ways. First, it enables teachers to engage with the moral and ethical aspects of education, including those that may surface in daily classroom life. Secondly, it means that teaching is not reduced to a set of practices rendering teachers as mere technicians in the classroom. Thirdly, it means that teachers can understand the contextual underpinnings of both the policy and practices that govern their work. In New Zealand, for example, the *New Zealand Curriculum* (Ministry of Education, 2007) has clear directives for the sorts of learners and citizens schools should be developing. As mandated education policy, it outlines the values and principles that teachers and schools are expected to model and reinforce. Becoming a teacher means thinking beyond the curriculum and wondering why the curriculum looks the way it does. What are the implications of the values and principles? What sorts of social vision does the curriculum promote? How does the curriculum construct the purposes of education? How does the curriculum shape teaching and learning?

This chapter argues for a certain type of philosophical space in initial teacher education, one that fosters philosophical questioning and thinking in sustained ways while learning to teach. What follows illustrates one possibility for doing this. It involves a process of *asking*, *examining*, and *becoming*:

1. *asking* searching questions about the aims and ideals of education;
2. *examining* philosophical responses to enduring questions in education; and
3. *becoming* a teacher who can apply philosophical questions and concepts to contemporary problems and issues in education, and whose practice can be defended against broader philosophical commitments to education.

## *Asking:* Enduring questions in education

I have argued that ideas matter in education because education can be conceived of as a set of competing and contested ideas. But to what extent should ideas matter to teachers? At a minimum, teachers should be able to understand the reasons why they do what they do. However, there is a more pressing reason why ideas should matter to teachers. This reason is connected to the role education can play in contributing to a fairer and more just society. Egan's (2001) claim that "we have the schools that we have because of the ideas that we hold", comes to this pointed conclusion: "If we want to improve our schools, it is the abstract and awkward realm of ideas that we must first deal with" (p. 940). That is, as we encounter educational problems, it is important to critically consider the underlying ideas and meanings actually at stake; for example, when debates about charter schools come up we understand that what we are actually doing is asking questions about the role of the state in relation to education. When we have debates about National Standards, we are asking questions about what the educated person should look like. When we have debates about curriculum we are asking questions about what knowledge is, and how we might select the best knowledge. When business and employers complain that schools are not producing work-ready youth, we are asking questions about the purposes of education. And, when we have debates about what preservice teachers need to know and be able to do, we are asking questions about what it means to teach.

If education has commitments to a greater common good, then the first point of reflection and questioning needs to be with the conceptions and meanings we hold about education. For preservice teachers, this can seem a futile task because philosophical questions often lack straightforward or singular answers. In her defence of philosophical approaches to education, Noddings (2007) asks whether we should concern ourselves with "questions that never go away" (p. 2). Her response is that philosophical questions grapple with issues present in every historical moment. Therefore, every historical moment requires an engagement with these questions, not necessarily in definitive ways, but in ways that help us clarify and understand present problems and challenges. Noddings' point, that philosophical questions are enduring, means philosophical thinking and questioning gives us insights about education by examining how people have addressed these questions in previous or different contexts from our own.

Moreover, philosophical questions are different from other types of questions in that they allow us to address questions that cannot be answered through empirical means (Noddings, 2007). While it is not possible to answer what the purposes of education are empirically, we can examine how historical meanings about education have shaped our current conceptions of education. From a rigorously informed position, we can then begin to advance our own arguments. In this view, philosophical thinking is an activity (Noddings, 2007) requiring active engagement from teachers. At the same time, philosophical thinking offers teachers more than just something to do; it also has the capacity to form teachers' professional identities in important ways. Greene (1977), for example, argues that to do philosophy is to "respond to actual problems and real interests, to the requirements of sense-making in a confusing world" (p. 123). All of this shifts us into a critical agency that allows us to engage with education and the broader world with a much deeper awareness.

What questions might we ask of education? As a starting point, we might begin with the following:

1. What are the aims of education?
2. What is teaching?
3. What does the educated person look like?
4. What is the best knowledge to teach?

And, because education ideals always embody human and societal ideals, it also means examining questions connected to wider society such as:

5. What kind of a society do we want to live in?
6. What kind of people do we want to be?
7. How might education enable these ideals?

One advantage of this type of questioning is that is also allows us to question normative claims made about education. Normative claims are pronouncements that assert how things ought to be. A contemporary example of a normative claim in education is that knowledge is quickly passing its use-by date and that schools should be more concerned with developing competencies and transferable skills than teaching content. This claim is made on the basis that the world is changing rapidly and we don't know what jobs will exist in the future. This is a largely uncontested claim and its assumed validity shapes contemporary discourse in powerful (and sometimes outrageous) ways. Yet we could, and should, interrogate this claim closely. For example, if we take our first question, "What are the aims of education?", we might refute this claim on the grounds that education serves a greater purpose than producing workers. If we make use of our fourth question, "What is the best knowledge to teach?", we might ask questions about how we ascribe value to knowledge and whether some forms of knowledge are actually in danger of soon becoming obsolete.

Normative claims abound in education and teachers should be able to address them in confident and rigorous ways. Whether you decide the claim is valid or not is not the important part, but it is knowing *why* you think it is valid (or not) that matters. This final point is critical because it suggests that becoming a teacher means being able to defend broader philosophical stances as well as everyday pedagogical choices. On similar grounds, McCann and Yaxley (2016) defend the importance of philosophical conversations in initial teacher education on the grounds that engaging in these conversations "offer[s] a critical commentary on the underpinning ideas which shape and influence the practice of schooling and education" (p. 69). Not only does this allow us to critically examine the multiple and competing narratives present in educational spaces, it also allows teachers to encounter a variety of viewpoints. A further affordance to teachers is they develop the means to infuse philosophical views in their professional practice and in their personal philosophies of teaching.

## *Examining: Ideas matter and they matter to teachers*

A thinking life requires us to examine education in its broadest sense. This means beyond the immediacy of the classroom and beyond the ideas that underpin education systems. Philosophers have responded to enduring questions about education in a variety of ways across multiple social and historical contexts. In this section, I take three questions from the list in the previous section and consider some philosophical responses. Each account represents a very brief introduction to some key concepts in the work of educational philosophers. Other chapters in this volume offer more extensive explanations of these and other philosophical positions. These brief accounts are also used to show how different conceptions of education lead to different possibilities for how we run our schools, what young people learn, and what teaching looks like. As you read through these examples, consider the extent to which these ideas are reflected in current curriculum documents and/or education discourses.

## 1. What are the aims of education? John Dewey and education as preparation for democratic living

John Dewey (1859–1952) wrote extensively about the relationship between education and democracy (Dewey, 1916; Noddings, 2007; Pring, 2007). His writings offer a clear illustration that education ideals are always connected to broader societal and human ideals. During his lifetime, Dewey witnessed immense social change, including ongoing debate about the relationship between school and society (Pring, 2007). His work is reflective of the important issues that dominated American life at the time; individualism, community, experience, and democracy are therefore prevailing themes in his work. One central idea in his educational philosophy is his conception of democracy as participation, or what he called *associated living*:

> A democracy is more than a form of government; it is primarily a mode of associated living, of conjoint communicated experience. (Dewey, 1916, p. 87)

By this, Dewey is describing a commitment to living in intentionally connected ways. In terms of education, Dewey saw schools as microcosms of society and therefore as instrumental in developing the dispositions necessary for collaborative community life. In accordance with his view of democracy as participation, Dewey sees the role of schools as fostering openness toward diversity and diverse views.

> A society which makes provision for participation in its good of all members on equal terms and which secures flexible readjustments of its institutions through interaction of the different forms of associated life is in so far democratic. Such a society must have a type of education which gives individuals a personal interest in social relationships and control, and the habits of mind which secure social changes without introducing disorder. (Dewey, 1916, p. 99)

The above quotation demonstrates Dewey's belief that education should play a role in maintaining the delicate balance between diverse views and shared commitments in society. Dewey's own commitment to both individualism *and* community is perhaps best expressed in his notion of the social individual. Dewey claims that individuals are social beings first and argues for a socially responsible individualism. In *My Pedagogic Creed—Article 1: What Education is* (1897) he argues that the role of education is to move individuals from a narrow, self-centred view of the world to one that is socially aware and responsible.

> I believe that the only true education comes through the stimulation of the child's powers by the demands of the social situations in which he finds himself. Through these demands he is stimulated to act as a member of a unity, to emerge from his original narrowness of action and feeling, and to conceive of himself from the standpoint of the welfare of the group to which he belongs. (Dewey, 1897, p. 1)

Another important idea in Dewey's conception of education is the centrality of experience (Pring, 2007). As the previous quotation illustrates, education occurs when learners are provided with appropriate experiential opportunities. Dewey's advocacy for learner-centred schools was a response to (then) traditional forms of schooling where students learned passively, individually, and under the authoritarian grasp of the teacher. Dewey argued for classrooms that resonated with students' lives, had practical applications, and provided opportunities to work in cooperative ways. The provision of suitable experiences is central to Dewey's philosophy, and for this reason Dewey saw the teacher's role as crucial to learning and growth.

From a Deweyan perspective, the aims of education are to foster the communicative dispositions for democratic living to flourish. Education should also lead to more learning and further growth. Dewey advocated for learner-centered classrooms in which learner interests were taken seriously, but this did not mean interests were pursued randomly. Rather, Dewey argued that teachers needed to play a central role in giving direction to these interests so that they led to a deeper understanding of human life in all its complexity.

## 2. What is the best knowledge to teach? A liberal philosophy of education

"What to teach?" is a central question in education and the issue of what should be included in school curricula persists in both policy and public discourse. Indeed, it is difficult to find someone who does *not* have an opinion about what should be taught in schools! Within a liberal philosophy of education, the main role of schooling is to develop rational autonomy (Alexander, 2008). This refers to people's ability to make their own choices in *reasoned and informed* ways. The reasoned and informed emphasis is important because it is tied to ideas about knowledge and to *which* forms of knowledge are most likely to deliver this type of agency. Significantly, the impetus for rational, autonomous individuals rests on the premise that liberal democratic societies require citizens who can exercise personal freedom (Alexander, 2008). This has important implications for education and for knowledge. First, if the role of education is to create independently thinking and acting individuals, then education must be freely available to all citizens. Secondly, it must provide all learners access to the same curriculum (Pring, 2007). Notions of the *common school* and a *common curriculum* are associated with a liberal philosophy of education.

From a liberal education perspective, the role of education is to discipline the mind with a view to engaging with the world in critically rigorous ways. Knowledge in the form of disciplines (knowledge organised into categories such as science or history) is central to this development. R. S. Peters (1919–2011) was a philosopher who is associated with this tradition and, for Peters, education and specific forms of knowledge lead to a "desirable state of mind".

> Education, then can have no end beyond itself, its value derives
> from principle and standards implicit upon it. To be educated is not
> to have arrived at a destination, but to travel with a different view.
> (Peters, 1967, p. 15)

The kind of knowledge that Peters advocates is distinct from experience (Peters, 1967). His view of knowledge is a markedly cognitive one involving the development of conceptual frameworks and understanding. Being educated is not merely learning a collection of facts or information, but the ability to understand and make sense within a particular disciplinary stance. For this reason, Peters saw education fundamentally as an initiation into disciplines. According to Peters, this disciplinary vantage point enables the development of principled and systematic approaches to knowledge. Formal education (as distinct from experience) allows learners to engage in systematic inquiry through the acquisition of disciplinary principles and methods for testing and producing knowledge. Peters' view of education as a *state of mind* is also suggestive of an overall orientation toward knowledge itself. Learners not only seek to study in systematic ways but develop a commitment and a pleasure in seeking knowledge this way.

A liberal philosophy of education addresses the question of knowledge in particular ways. It privileges a cognitive view of knowledge organised into distinct disciplines. The place of these distinct knowledge forms is central to education because they enable the development of habits of mind. These habits of mind foster autonomous and informed participation in society. From this perspective, knowledge is seen as intellectual capital, and therefore access to a broad knowledge base is a fundamental aspect of democratic society. In this school of thought the best knowledge to teach is a broad disciplinary knowledge base.

### 3. What is teaching? Paulo Freire and the teacher as ethical and political agent

Brazilian educator Paulo Freire (1921–1997) began his work in education by developing literacy programmes for the poorest and most dispossessed people in Brazil (Roberts, 2000). Throughout his work, Freire maintained that education was not neutral but a political act (Freire, 1997, 2005). His assertion that education has the capacity to oppress or to liberate has significant implications for teachers and teaching (Freire & Shor, 1987). For Freire, teachers can never be neutral, and he argued that teachers must always decide "in favour of whom" they are teaching (Freire & Shor, 1987). Freire saw claims of neutrality on behalf of teachers as siding with oppression (Freire, 1997). This is because education involves things such as selecting knowledge, deciding who learns what, how, and to what end. It is also a series of power relations between teachers and students, schools and communities, policy makers, the state, and the education sector. This situates the teacher at an important intersection between various contexts; inevitably, teaching means making choices.

Freire's claim that education is not neutral but a political act locates his philosophy in a Marxist tradition (Roberts, 2000). As such, he is concerned with power relationships and how they might be sustained and reproduced in educational institutions and practices. It follows then that the pedagogy he advocates encourages students to engage in a structural analysis of society. This includes examining institutional structures and encouraging students to identify personal problems as public issues.

A good illustration of this pedagogy is Freire's literacy work. Freire's initial literacy work in the slums of Brazil involved teaching people how to read and write at a time when only those who could read had the right to vote. In this social context, literacy—as the means to equal democratic participation—*is* justice. Freire began by identifying vocabulary that emerged from people's lives alongside pictures illustrating their material conditions. This then generated dialogue aimed at describing social reality. Here the role of education is to create political awareness among learners in order to liberate them from structures that oppress them.

Similarly, Freire's problem-posing education seeks to reconcile what Freire called the student/teacher contradiction. Freire argues that traditional forms of schooling and education simply reproduce unequal power relationships in society through a *banking* model of education (Freire, 1997). By this he is referring to the way in which students are largely passive recipients of the knowledge that teachers *give* to them. Banking education, according to Freire, is domesticating because it teaches learners to be subservient. It teaches them that unequal power relationships are an expected part of life and not to challenge authority or critique what they are given. In both literacy work and in problem-posing education the teacher plays an important role working alongside students in solidarity with them.

Freire's response to the question "What is teaching?" is that teaching is a human endeavour as opposed to a technical or practical one (Freire, 2005). Framing of teaching as a political act means that teachers must inevitably choose whether to maintain or to work against social injustice. Freire's own pedagogical approaches to teaching and learning show his own commitment to structural change through education. For teachers, Freire advocates *praxis* as a way not only to reflect critically but to commit to action in order to bring about change (1998). He identifies necessary teacher qualities as humility, love, tolerance, decisiveness, and a "patient impatience" (Freire, 2005). These qualities speak to the human element that Freire saw as an inescapable part of teaching.

## *Becoming: Committing to a thinking life*

I have outlined the value of philosophical questioning and examined some philosophical responses to three enduring questions in education. In this final section I discuss what committing to a thinking life can mean in relation to becoming a teacher. The professional identity advocated for in this chapter is one requiring an engagement with education in its broadest sense. There are (at least) two ways this deep engagement can manifest itself in teachers' lives. One is that teachers commit to examining contemporary education puzzles and challenges using philosophical ideas and questions. The other is that teachers develop personal teaching and learning philosophies which are justified against broader commitments to education.

### 1. Using philosophical concepts to engage with educational issues

**What would Dewey say about charter schools?**

Given that Dewey thought the curriculum should have practical application and emerge from students' interests, would he think charter schools were a good idea? Charter schools are supposed to provide more choice for students by having more freedom to design purpose-built curricula to meet a variety of needs. In Auckland, one example is the Vanguard Military Academy where some traditional subjects are taught in a military-style setting. On the one hand, we could say that Dewey would welcome the innovation and the desire to meet the needs of students who are not being served by mainstream education. On the other hand, Dewey might question the school's military ethos and its ability to foster democratic dispositions in students. How would Dewey's concept of *associated living, growth, and/or experience* sit with the school? To what extent does the school foster the sorts of active participation needed for democratic living? Is his view that teachers should be guides rather than taskmasters (Pring, 2007) consistent with the school's approach? Dewey's insistence that education should engage student interest and have practical application is an argument still pertinent today. It is likely he would have much to say about charter schools. By making use of his concepts we can critically consider this kind of schooling against broader education ideals.

## What would Freire say about shifting preservice teacher education from universities and into schools?

Presently initial teacher education is under scrutiny and reform in Aotearoa New Zealand. Ministry of Education initiatives include new programmes such as Teach First NZ and the Master of Teaching. These new programmes have an emphasis on practice and involve extended time in schools. This focus on practice is sometimes connected to the idea that teaching should be viewed as an apprenticeship, and that on-the-job training in schools is the best way to train teachers. What position might Freire adopt in relation to shifting preservice teacher education into schools and having a stronger focus on practice? Freire maintained that it is important for teachers to work in solidarity with their students. Would extended opportunities in schools be more likely to foster better understanding of student lives and material conditions than they would from a removed university environment? Or might Freire be concerned that a shift to practice reduces teaching to methods and skills with limited opportunities to critique education policy and structures? How might his concepts of *concientization* and/or *banking education* be useful in this analysis? What kind of preservice teacher education would be consistent with Freire's vision of teaching?

## How might we respond to National Standards and high-stakes testing from a liberal knowledge perspective?

New Zealand's education system is often described as a high quality but low equity system. A close analysis of PISA[1] data makes for concerning reading in terms of the disparity in student achievement. This has led to an intense focus on ways to close the achievement gap between different groups of students. One way in which policy has sought to do this has been to increase testing and benchmark setting, including the introduction of National Standards in 2011. One critique of this measure is that students who are struggling to meet the standards will experience a "narrower curriculum" as their teachers focus on getting them to the required literacy and numeracy standards.

---

1 PISA (Programme for International Student Assessment) is an international assessment of the knowledge and skills of 15-year-olds. New Zealand is one of the countries that takes part every 3 years.

A liberal philosophy of education views equal access to a broad knowledge base as a fundamental aspect of an equitable society. Inasmuch as access to a wide range of disciplinary thinking develops the capacity for critical engagement, liberal philosophers of education advocate for the centrality of knowledge in education. How might we respond to policy such as National Standards from a liberal perspective? Is it possible to defend the Standards on the grounds they ensure all students have the basics of reading, writing, and mathematics?

## 2. Developing a personal teaching and learning philosophy

Teaching philosophies are useful because they provide a basis for justifying practice (Grant & Sleeter, 2007). While it is possible to develop a philosophy with a focus solely on methods and skills, a broad philosophy draws links between pedagogical commitments and the wider purposes of education. This is a much wider encompassing professional identity, one that demonstrates intellectual engagement with education. Grant and Sleeter (2007) draw on Garforth's (1964, in Grant & Sleeter, 2007) work to outline the benefits of a broad teaching philosophy. A broad philosophy helps teachers to:

1. Bring new interpretations to old problems;
2. Evaluate and think critically about traditional or sanctioned ideas;
3. Respond in ways that are ethical;
4. Respond in ways that are consistent with your values;
5. Develop reflective and critical capacities, always interrogating ideas and practices rather than just accepting them as sanctioned truth. (Grant & Sleeter, 2007, p. 17)

This chapter represents various ideological stances connected to broader aims and commitments in society. The *New Zealand Curriculum* (*NZC*) (Ministry of Education, 2007) provides one example of a philosophy underpinned by a broader commitment to the purposes of education. It outlines a particular social vision for learners in Aotearoa New Zealand. The *NZC* is foregrounded by a mission, a vision, principles, values, and key competencies. The main stated purpose of the *NZC* is for learners to be "actively contributing and participating members of society" (Ministry of Education, 2007, p. 8). It could be argued that the *NZC* upholds participatory democracy as a desired outcome of education. How then, might you develop a personal philosophy that encompasses these ideas? How does one teach for participatory democracy? What sorts of practices and/or curriculum choices are most likely to lead to this outcome?

## Conclusion

All ideas have their own geographies. They have their own contours and configurations that make education landscapes possible. Philosophical thinking allows us to navigate these landscapes and encounter education anew as rich conceptual terrain. It offers teachers "conceptual agilities" providing a much broader space for thought and action to negotiate school life (McCann & Yaxley, 2016, p. 70). Becoming a teacher is about giving meaning to education through thoughtful engagement with abstract and *awkward* ideas. Education is not static or complete, nor can empirical methods address all issues and problems associated with it. Instead we breathe life into education by constructing and reconstructing responses to enduring questions and challenges. In this sense, we might say education is an idea teachers make up on a daily basis in their classrooms. Egan (2001, p. 939) encourages us to abandon problematic conceptions of education, and "make up" new ones but this requires a robust framework to work from. Philosophical thinking provides us with this framework and enables us to address a fundamental question for classroom teachers: "What meanings will *I* give to education?" True story.

## References

Alexander, H. (2008). What is common about schooling? Rational autonomy and moral agency in liberal democratic education. In R. Pring, M. Halstead, G. Haydon (Eds.), *The common school and the comprehensive ideal: A defence by Richard Pring with complementary essays* (pp.108–123). Chichester, UK: Wiley-Blackwell.

Clark, J. (2004). The ethics of teaching and the teaching of ethics. *New Zealand Journal of Teachers' Work, 1*(2), 80–84.

Barnett, R. (2009). Knowing and becoming in the higher education curriculum. *Studies in Higher Education 34*(4): 429–440.

Dewey, J. (1897). *My pedagogic creed*. Retrieved from *https://en.wikisource.org/wiki/ My_Pedagogic_Creed*

Dewey, J. (1916). *Democracy and education*. New York, NY: Macmillan.

Egan, K. (2001). Why education is so difficult and contentious. *Teachers College Record, 103*(6), 923–941.

Freire, P. (1997). *Pedagogy of the oppressed*. New York, NY: Continuum.

Freire, P. (2005). *Teachers as cultural workers: Letters to those who dare to teach*. Cambridge, MA: Westview Press.

Freire, P., & Shor, I. (1987). *A pedagogy for liberation: Dialogues on transforming education*. South Hadley, MA: Bergin & Garvey.

Grant, C. A., & Sleeter, C. E. (2007). *Doing multicultural education for achievement and equity*. New York, NY: Routledge.

Greene, M. (1977). Toward wide-awakeness: An argument for the arts and the humanities in education. *Teachers College Record. 79*(1), 119–125.

McCann, H. & Yaxley, B., (2016). Retaining the philosophy of education in teacher education. In M. Peters & M. Tesar (Eds.), *In search of subjectivities: An educational philosophy and theory teacher education reader* pp. (67–83). London and New York: Routledge.

Ministry of Education. (2007). *The New Zealand curriculum*. Wellington: Learning Media.

Noddings, N. (2007). *Philosophy of education*. (2nd ed.). Boulder, CO: Westview Press.

Peters, R. S. (1967). Education as initiation. In R. S. Peters (Ed.), *The concept of education* (pp. 1–23). London, UK: Routledge & Kegan Paul.

Pring, R. (2007). *John Dewey: A philosopher of education for our time?* London, UK: Continuum International.

Roberts, P. (2000). *Education, literacy, and humanization: Exploring the work of Paulo Freire*. Westport, CN: Bergin & Garvey.

## Introduction  Discussion starters

1. Gómez states that becoming a teacher is not the same as learning to teach. What does she mean by this? Do you agree with her observation? Justify your response.

2. What beliefs about teaching and learning are already part of your emerging personal philosophy of teaching? Where did these ideas come from? Who has influenced your thinking?

3. What are some of the issues confronting education today that require deeper examination? How might thinking philosophically help make sense of these issues?

4. Various writers talk of teaching being a *moral* or *political* act. What do they mean by this? Can you think of examples of when, as a teacher, you might face a moral or political conundrum? How might you navigate your way through?

TRADITION 1: PROGRESSIVISM

# Progressivism—a personal reflection

Peter O'Connor

*School of Critical Studies in Education*
*Faculty of Education and Social Work*
*The University of Auckland*

## *The times they haven't changed*

One of the dangers in getting older is withdrawal into a romanticised rewriting of personal and social history. This leads into the 'no man's land' of castigating the present by suggesting that, in the rainbow-hued world of the past, it was all so much better. The danger, therefore, of looking back at what might be thought of as the progressive education era is that we become passively nostalgic. Progressivism was a reforming agenda to change schools from a system designed more to punish children than to liberate them into a life of learning. The progressive movement never reached its full potential but, looking back now when the last vestiges of it are being eroded in New Zealand schools, I am filled not so much with nostalgia but a slow, burning anger at the damage being done.

I still struggle to imagine New Zealand in 1937, when a series of conferences, led by 14 distinguished international education academics, could attract the thousands who came to listen, discuss and then implement a new pedagogical contract for schools that would last for generations. The New Education Fellowship events heralded the beginning of what was referred to as both *progressive* and *new* education. They were to be the cornerstones of the official policy of schooling in New Zealand for over 50 years.

In the era of the First Labour Government (elected in 1935, at the heart of the Great Depression), progressive education needs to be understood as part of a wider agenda of progressive politics being enacted by the government. The notions that human history was malleable, that the economic and social disasters of the 1930s could be ameliorated by the state, and that government had a responsibility to enact laws that reduced inequality, were part of the policies that drove the reforming government. Education was vital to their policies and plans to lift people out of poverty and to improve their life chances.

In the midst of the global depression, marginalised groups were increasingly attracted to fundamentalist and dehumanising ideologies. Fascism and Stalinism drew support for their easy and slippery answers from the poor and dislocated who saw redemption from their misery in the demagoguery of leaders who played on fears, teased out innate racism, and traded on ignorance.

Progressive politics and, in particular, progressive education were vital in the 1930s as a counter-measure to the anti-democratic impulses of the times. The intellectual heart-spring of progressive education was the writings of John Dewey. Dewey (1916) understood the vital link between public education and democracy. A critically informed population who were capable, not merely of answering questions, but who could question answers as well were seen as a front line of defence for participatory democracy. Dewey argued education should be valued because it was a public good. Dewey's thinking deeply influenced Peter Fraser, New Zealand's most visionary Minister of Education, and Dr Clarence Beeby, its most charismatic Director of Education. They were the country's most ideologically driven leaders of education until the appointment of Hekia Parata.

Central to progressive education was the oft-cited statement by Peter Fraser that:

> The Government's objective, broadly expressed, is that all persons, whatever their ability, rich or poor, whether they live in town or country, have a right as citizens to a free education of the kind for which they are best fitted and to the fullest extent of their powers. So far is this from being a mere pious platitude that the full acceptance of the principle will involve the reorientation of the education system. (Fraser, 1939, as cited in Maharey, 2003, n.p.)

Fraser, with this statement, affirms a public good and right-of-citizenship basis for the reforms that he and Beeby were to put in place. Beeby put it less poetically than Fraser when he said the reforms were about "making the education system responsive to the needs of the individual kid" (Maharey, 2003). The system they were replacing was heavy on national testing, a filtering system that regularly deemed children failures, and, in particular, denied access to higher education to the poor and to Māori. In its place, Beeby fought for a system that, as I was reminded as I trained as a teacher in the 1970s, was about "starting where the kids are at".

Play and the arts became part of the New Zealand education system in a way that is hard to imagine in the cold and sterile environment of education in the 21st century classroom. The arts were seen as important because the progressives understood that the social imaginary was a necessary step in the protection of democracy. Being able to imagine that you don't have to die in the world into which you are born, that you can reinvent yourself—and, more importantly, the world—in the interests of social justice, was seen as the contribution the arts could make to both schooling and the nation. Progressive educators understood the importance of embodied learning (that true, deep learning requires more than the manipulation of fingers and a screen). They understood that it was in the physical making of real things that learning could arise from experience. The work of arts educators including Gordon Tovey, Elwyn Richardson, and Arnold Manaaki Wilson (Beiringa & Beiringa, 2015; MacDonald, 2016) are some of the greatest examples of the power of arts education anywhere in the world.

The neoliberal reforms of *Tomorrow's Schools* (Lange, 1988) began the process of dismantling progressive education. The goal of public good was sold away to a system that focuses almost entirely on individual achievement and the acquisition of a narrowly defined set of skills for participation in a low-wage economy. As part of the great state asset-stripping of the 1980s, public education was just another commodity to be bought and sold in the marketplace. Schools were reduced to competing business units.

Eighty years after the introduction of the progressive era in New Zealand we again see a world torn apart by rising inequality and poor and uneducated people manipulated by demagogues. We see again a world where dehumanising and fundamentalist approaches are attractive to the young and the displaced. But, instead of embracing an education system that acts to counter these trends, in this country we are stripping the potential of the social imagination from our students, and closing off access to disciplinary knowledge with a focus on skills teaching. We are returning to a focus on the test as a sorting system even though government rhetoric argues it is to lift underachievement. We risk democracy itself when we lose sight of public education as a national treasure.

The great gift of progressivism is that it centres on hope—not hope for personal advancement and the accretion of individual wealth, but for the public good. Instead, it asserts a belief that the world might be better, safer, more democratic, less constrained by bigots and leaders of false hope. Progressivism reminds us there is more to education than preparation for the future of work. Progressivism claims there remains possibility in the world, possibility for social justice, possibilities for change.

## References

Beiringa, J. (Producer) & Bieringa, L (Director). (2016). *The HeART of the matter.* [Documentary film]. BWX Productions.

Dewey J. (1916). *Democracy and education: An introduction to the philosophy of education.* New York, NY: Macmillan.

Dewey, J. (1934). *Art as experience.* New York, NY: Macmillan.

Lange, D. (1988). *Tomorrow's schools: The reform of education administration in New Zealand.* Wellington: Government Printer.

MacDonald, M. (2016). *Elwyn Richardson and the early world of creative education in New Zealand.* Wellington: NZCER Press.

Maharey, S. (2003). *The Beeby vision today* [Speech]. Retrieved from https://www.beehive.govt.nz/speech/beeby-vision-today

PROGRESSIVISM—HISTORY AND CONCEPTS

# Chapter 2 Understanding progressive education and its influence on policy and pedagogy in New Zealand

Carol Mutch

*School of Critical Studies in Education*
*Faculty of Education and Social Work*
*The University of Auckland*

**Abstract**

*Progressive education* is a term that can polarise people. It could be seen as a way of engaging children in authentic and meaningful learning or it could be seen as merely encouraging children to play or undertake *busy work* without gaining any substantive knowledge. In order to understand these different perspectives, it helps to return to the roots of progressive education—what was it in response to and what did it set out to do differently? It is then useful to examine how it was implemented over time and in different contexts—in particular in New Zealand where it has had a profound influence on the development of educational policy and pedagogy since the 1930s. This chapter introduces the history and legacy of progressive education through the eyes and experiences of a progressive teacher.

**Key words**
Progressive education—child-centred—holistic education—pedagogy

## *The early development of progressive education*
While some writers might consider that the seeds of progressive educational ideas were sown by philosophers such as John Locke (1632–1704), who felt that learning came from perception, observation and experience, I want to start with those who explored these ideas more fully in educational settings. One of the first of these was Jean-Jacques Rousseau (1712–1778), who described a learner-centred education in his book, *Emile, or On Education* (1762). The hypothetical Emile is to be taught in the countryside and learn through observation and investigation. He will be guided by a tutor who arranges appropriate learning experiences. In this treatise on education are some of the threads of what was to become progressive education—experiential learning, naturalistic settings, developmentally appropriate learning, and the teacher as facilitator. Emile will not be subject to punishment but will learn the consequences of his actions through experience. Thus, we get an understanding of what this new approach was reacting to—traditional formal settings that encouraged rote learning and stifled creativity, with harsh punishment for those students who did not obey or fit the mould. It is important to note, however, that Rousseau outlined this education only for Emile. Sophie, who was destined to marry Emile, would be prepared for a domestic life as Emile's helpmate. Mary Wollstonecraft (1759–1797), an early feminist, was to critique this view of women in her book, *A Vindication of the Rights of Woman* (1792).

A further development of child-centred ideals appears in the work of Johann Pestalozzi (1746–1827). He considered that learning was a holistic activity that encompassed all aspects of a child's life—head, hand, and heart. He designed specific lessons where children learned through their senses and by the study and manipulation of objects. He set up schools in Switzerland and Germany to put these ideas into practice and his teaching methods attracted interest from throughout Europe and the United States. His schools included physical and outdoor activities alongside the careful study of objects to build conceptual understanding. Friedrich Froebel (1782–1852), the founder of kindergartens, was a student of Pestalozzi. Froebel believed that children were not just miniature adults, but had unique needs, interests, and capabilities. In his kindergartens (children's gardens), very young children were encouraged to find self-expression through play. He wanted their imaginations to be stimulated through songs and stories and their ideas to be expressed through creative activities and the arts. He also felt that learning to work together through games was important for social development.

In the period from the mid-18th century to the late 19th century, we see the beginnings and evolution of many ideas that have filtered into today's classrooms and early childhood centres. They were a reaction to traditional teaching methods and in response to evolving ideas about the nature of childhood. The next period, from the late 19th century until the mid-20th century, saw the embedding of some of these ideas into mainstream early childhood education and formal schooling.

In Europe, Rudolph Steiner (1869–1925) extended the idea of teaching the whole child through the development of the philosophy that underpinned his Waldorf schools. He prepared a developmentally appropriate curriculum which was differentiated into three levels: early childhood, with an emphasis on hands-on activities and creative expression; primary, with an emphasis on social and artistic development; and secondary, with a focus on developing critical reasoning and intellectual ability. Topics were taught in a more integrated, multi-disciplinary manner. Maria Montessori (1870–1952), who was later to be nominated twice for a Nobel Peace Prize, founded her first Casa dei Bambini (children's house) in 1907. She set up a prepared learning environment with child-sized furniture and activities to encourage children to explore and follow up lines of interest. Teachers were expected to balance structured routines with free and expressive play.

In the United States, John Dewey (1859–1952), perhaps the best known progressive educator, began his career as a teacher but soon moved to academia where he began to think and write about the nature of teaching and learning (see, for example, *The School and Society*, 1899; *Experience and Education*, 1938). Dewey agreed with earlier progressive ideas that children were not to be treated as passive recipients of knowledge but, instead, engaged in the active, hands-on processing of material. He promoted learning through direct contact with the environment, solving practical problems and thinking critically—ideas that still exist today in experiential learning, problem-based learning, and inquiry learning. While at the University of Chicago, he ran a laboratory school which enabled him to experiment with his version of progressive pedagogy. Dewey's ideas were never implemented system-wide, yet Dewey was often seen as "responsible" for developments in progressive education by both its proponents and detractors. Dewey raised concerns about taking progressivism to extremes and noted that education should be a balance between being child-led and curriculum-led. He saw teaching as a social act with an ethical and moral purpose. He felt that schools, as social institutions, were well placed to prepare children and young people for their place in a democratic society.

Perhaps the most concrete example of progressive education pushing the boundaries was undertaken at Summerhill. A.S. Neill (1883–1973) became interested in the *Neue Schule* (New School) movement in Europe in the early 1920s. He set up his own version in England in 1924 before moving to its present site in Suffolk in 1927. The co-educational boarding school was run on democratic lines where children had an equal voice in decision making. It freed children from a set curriculum and any imposed routines. The following statement is from the school's current website[2]:

> Summerhill is a school of personal choice, where students must decide each day how they will use their time … they can play, they can involve themselves in a variety of constructive social situations, they can be by themselves to read or daydream, they can engage in self directed group projects and activities, and they can choose to attend formal lessons … each day the children define themselves by choice and action … this is a profound experience that leads to a strong sense of personal and responsibility and self knowledge.

Summerhill did not always meet with the approval of the authorities and, in the 1950s, school numbers were at their lowest ebb. With the publication of the philosophy behind the school in the 1960s, A.S. Neill's ideas gained more widespread respect (see, Neill, 1962). The school still operates today with around 75 students.

---

[2] www.summerhillschool.co.uk/learning-at-summerhill.php

## *The characteristics of progressive education*

In order to understand why progressive education flourished, it helps to understand the differences between traditional education in the 18th and 19th centuries and what progressive educators were aiming to achieve. In Table 2.1, the differences are displayed across different domains—namely, the purpose of education, the setting for learning, beliefs about learning, the nature of the child, the role of the teacher, activities for learning, and the assessment of learning. In the nature of such syntheses, Table 2.1 makes broad generalisations and the two approaches appear as opposites when, in fact, the reality was varied and fluid. It serves, however, to highlight what progressive educators considered they were reacting against.

Table 2.1. *Differences between traditional and progressive education in the 19th century*

| Characteristics | Traditional education | Progressive education |
| --- | --- | --- |
| *The purpose of education* | To fill vacant minds with knowledge<br><br>To instil discipline into children | To instil a love of nature and learning<br><br>To allow children's individuality and creativity to flourish |
| *The setting for learning* | In classrooms where children sat in rows (and, in some cases, in rank order of achievement) | In naturalistic settings, such as the outdoors, or in flexible learning spaces with a range of sensory stimuli |
| *Beliefs about learning* | Learning was a passive activity that required uncritical uptake of what was presented | Learning was an active process that required engagement in the world around the students and with teachers and peers |
| *The nature of the child* | Children were adults-in-the-making<br><br>Children needed to be moulded carefully and monitored strictly | Childhood had its own unique needs and characteristics<br><br>Children were inherently good and this needed to be nurtured |
| *The role of the teacher* | The teacher was the holder and distiller of knowledge | The teacher was a guide or facilitator, providing accessible materials and activities |
| *Activities for learning* | Learning by rote, repetition and copying<br><br>Observation of the teacher demonstrating a procedure or experiment | Learning activities used all the senses and engaged the body, the mind and the imagination |
| *Assessment of learning* | Regurgitating facts through recitation or examination<br><br>Exact replication of experiments or artefacts | The process of learning was as important as the outcomes<br><br>Individualised expression and interpretation were encouraged |

## *The development of progressive education in New Zealand*

While Māori, the first arrivals in New Zealand, had an education system that was communally based and prepared children and young people for the roles they would play in Māori society, the later arrival of settlers from Europe brought different educational traditions and assumptions. These included more formal and structured schooling, often in age cohorts, conducted in settings removed from everyday life.

Establishing universal primary education in New Zealand began with the Education Act of 1877, which established a system of free, compulsory and secular schooling. The first school syllabus included a broad base of knowledge and skills, from the 3Rs, grammar, and composition, to geography, science, drawing, and music. The secondary curriculum remained more traditional and elitist until the early 1900s when secondary schooling was made more accessible by offering vocational subjects as well as academic disciplines. Naturalistic and progressive educational theories were beginning to make their impact on the schooling system. George Hogben (1853–1920), Inspector General of Schools, championed free secondary education and was strongly influenced by Froebel and Rousseau:

> We must believe with Froebel and others of the most enlightened of the world's educators, that the child will learn best, not so much by reading about things in books as by doing: that is exercising his natural activities by making things, by observing and testing things for himself; and then afterwards reasoning about them and expressing thoughts about them. (Hogben, as cited in May, 2011, p. 37)

Early childhood establishments were also needed in the new colony. Crèches, such as those organised by Mother Aubert (1835–1926) and the Sisters of Compassion, cared for children whose mothers worked, but they were based on child care rather than education. As ideas from Rousseau, Pestalozzi, and Froebel filtered through, there was heightened interest in educating the whole child. The first kindergarten was established in Dunedin in 1889. Kindergartens were to support stay-at-home mothers and promoted play, physical activities, and preparation for school. Montessori preschools followed in the early 1900s. With the establishment of the Plunket Society, children's health and welfare became a higher priority and parents were encouraged to realise the benefits of getting children out to play in the fresh air and sunlight.

Although World War I interrupted the pace of change, there were continuing pockets of progressivism. Following the 1919 influenza epidemic, for example, the physical layout of schools was reconsidered based on experimental open-air classrooms in the UK, championed by Professor James Shelley (1884–1961) at Canterbury University and the Christchurch Open-Air League. The Canterbury Education Board was persuaded to try open-air classrooms. In 1924, Fendalton School in Christchurch was rebuilt with new classrooms which had folding doors to let in the sun and wide verandahs which allowed lessons to be conducted in the fresh air.

The impact of the Great Depression, beginning in the late 1920s, was to further stall progress and it was not until the First Labour Government swept to victory in 1935 that progressive ideals in education really took hold. The new Government promised a fairer and more just society and undertook social and educational reform on a grand scale. Peter Fraser (1884–1950), first as Minister of Education and later as Prime Minister, was responsible for much of the social reform and, through his work with Clarence Beeby (1902–1998), for major developments in education. Abbiss (1998) notes, "This association would facilitate educational reform in the 1930s and establish progressive education as the new orthodoxy" (p. 83). Beeby also served on the planning committee for the 1937 New Education Fellowship Conference, which would bring the latest in progressive educational thought to New Zealand.

The New Education Fellowship (NEF) was an organisation with its origins in Europe in the aftermath of World War I. It advocated a schooling system predicated on many progressive ideals: schooling should be holistic, democratic, creative and expressive. In 1937, progressive education speakers from around the world were brought to New Zealand. The NEF Conference captured the interest of educators, politicians, and the general public. It was broadcast around the country and the school holidays were changed to allow teachers to attend. Alcorn (1999) elaborates:

Those who were there remembered the feeling of inspiration: the sense that education was of crucial importance, that it was a liberating force, that home and school would work together, that education could and should be an active process." (p. 84)

Beeby went on to become Director of Education and to make further changes: in order to make secondary schooling more accessible, it became free until the age of 19; to ease the transition between primary and secondary schooling, the number of intermediate schools was increased; and the Proficiency Examination, which limited entry to secondary school, was abolished. In primary schools, class sizes were reduced, leading to the need for more schools, classrooms, and teachers as education achieved a sense of urgency.

Fraser and Beeby were a formidable team and are best remembered for the following statement which became the cornerstone of educational philosophy for many years:

The Government's objective, broadly expressed, is that every person whatever his level of academic ability, whether he be rich or poor, whether he live in town or country, has a right as a citizen, to a free education of the kind for which he is best fitted, and to the fullest extent of his powers. (As cited in Alcorn, 1999, p. 99)

Beeby was keen to give innovative educators a chance to flourish. One of the teachers he visited to see progressive education in practice was Elwyn Richardson (1925–2012), a teacher at Oruaiti School in an isolated part of Northland. The arts, and in particular, working with clay, were the catalyst for learning in Richardson's school, as children moved between different expressive activities (see, Richardson, 1964; MacDonald, 2016). Another teacher who was able to flourish in this progressive climate was Sylvia Ashton-Warner (1908–1984). Her books about teaching in remote Māori schools (such as *Teacher*, 1963) outline her method for teaching reading and writing based on children's interests through "key vocabulary"—words that held special significance for each child.

In the field of early childhood, progressive educators were also encouraging children to observe the world around them, engage in creative play and use that as a basis for their learning. Parent-led services, such as the Playcentre movement, which drew inspiration from the

NEF and the work of Susan Issacs (1885–1948), began in the early 1940s, led in part by Beeby's wife, Beatrice.

Progressive education even influenced the more rigid secondary system. The Thomas Report of 1944 introduced a common core curriculum (of English, mathematics, science, social studies, art, music, and physical education) into the first 2 years of secondary schooling, delaying subject specialisation until students sat the national School Certificate examination in their third year.

A progressive philosophy was to underpin education in early childhood centres and primary schools and, to a lesser extent, the first 2 years of secondary school, for the next three decades but it was not without its critics.

## *Critiques of progressive education*

Critiques of progressivism surfaced in the US in the 1930s and reached a peak in the 1950s when it became the "whipping boy" (Ozmon, 1965, p. 169) for all that was wrong with education. Traditionalists decried the loss of a classical education and religious conservatives blamed schools for a loss of morals. Critiques of progressive education were often stated in strong terms, "… progressive educationists oppose drilling, memorizing and hard work" (Reedy, n.d., p. 6). Critics claimed that direct teaching was dismissed in favour of play, subject matter was rejected, a cumulative and sequential curriculum disregarded, mastery ignored, competition eliminated, and core subjects pushed aside by fads. One of the more extreme statements claimed "… hairdressing and embalming are just as important, if not a little more so, than history and philosophy" (Mortimer Smith, as cited in Evers, 1998).

Similar concerns arose in New Zealand. Cumming and Cumming, discussing the media's criticism of education's "playway" methods in the 1950s, note:

> So much attention was given to it by the country's press that readers mistook all criticism for condemnation. It became fashionable for employers to be appalled at the declining standards of writing and spelling; they claimed that the basic standards of education had been discarded. (1978, p. 336)

In 1960, the Labour Government appointed the Currie Commission to review education. The review found, in fact, that there was a sound body of theory underlying educational practice and, while they did recommend changes, these were in the end too numerous and expensive to implement.

The 1960s and 1970s, however, saw a resurgence in progressive ideas. Tamariki School in Christchurch, based on the free school concept (best exemplified by Summerhill), was established in 1966. More integrated and progressive curriculum initiatives from the US, the UK, and Europe spread to New Zealand and were adopted to some extent. "New maths" attempted to take a more holistic approach to teaching mathematics for understanding by using set theory and transformational geometry rather than through the rote learning of arithmetic tables and formulae. "New social studies" integrated history and geography and drew on sociology, anthropology, and economics to create a thematic approach to understanding society. The Nuffield Science Project encouraged teachers to teach science using a hands-on, inquiry approach. While these initiatives were influential for a time, they came under much criticism, especially from parents, whose own education had been much different. It was at this time that I trained as teacher.

## Reflecting on my time as a progressive teacher

I left Teachers' College brimming with progressive ideas. I was going to develop teaching units around children's interests and integrate learning across the curriculum. I was going to fill my classroom with books, read poetry aloud every day, use group work in mathematics, and find ways to get outside the classroom walls as often as possible. And did I succeed? Mostly. Much of my teaching was in intermediate schools. While students would go to specialist teachers for music, science, physical education, and manual training (cooking and sewing for girls; woodwork and metalwork for boys), for the rest of the day we could immerse ourselves in our chosen topics. In my first class, we studied advertising. We plastered the classroom walls up to the ceiling (in the days before health and safety regulations) with magazine and newspaper advertisements to illustrate how advertising was all-pervasive. For maths, we graphed types, numbers, and target audiences of advertisements. In language, we studied the persuasive and literary techniques used to encourage us to part with our money. In social studies and science, we investigated the social harm and health effects of different products. I felt we were fully engaged in active learning but, when the school inspector came, he thought that I needed to improve my classroom control and spend more time marking students' exercise books.

At a different intermediate school, we undertook a study where the class was set up as a community—students devised identities and roles, designed their homes, set up budgets, organised businesses and infrastructure, wrote for their community newspaper, held elections for the local council and, when a motorway threatened to divide their town, undertook a protest campaign. Another teacher complained when my class marched around the school grounds at lunchtime with their placards, chanting, "No way, motorway!"

At a different school, a primary school this time, in a state housing area (what would later be termed a *low-decile school*) where I was teaching 7-year-olds, one child said he had never been to the beach. That sparked "Water Week". We went to the beach, the aquarium, the big swimming pool in the city, the wharf—and, purely by chance, a submarine was in port and we were allowed to go on board. Transport was arranged by parents who borrowed big vans (in the days before risk-management checklists and staff–student ratios). Back at school, we studied the water cycle, set up a rain gauge, did experiments with water, painted, wrote, and sang about water. I still have a photograph of the boy who had never been to the beach with the biggest smile on his face.

On reflection, how would I describe my teaching? Was it all play with no substance? In fact, no. I think I epitomised New Zealand's "liberal-progressive" tradition rather than pure progressivism. In order for education to liberate the individual, to expand their horizons and prepare them for later life, I had to balance "doing" with "knowing". It was not enough to just do exciting, fun, and messy things—they had to have a point. Activities needed to teach students more about the world, to build on the knowledge they already had, to make connections across the curriculum, and to prepare them for the next stages of learning. In order to get the most out of student-centred learning, it could not just be left to chance, students needed a sound foundation of knowledge and skill. This might require concentrated reading, focused teaching, individual study or even rote learning to reach a level of competence and confidence to engage in deeper personal learning. At the same time, I did not want learning for learning's sake. If students could see a use or a reason, if it resonated with something they were familiar with or curious about, it would be more engaging and authentic. Finding examples of the Fibonacci sequence in nature made numbers on a page come alive; studying the gorse bushes in the back paddock made the life cycle of an insect more intimately observable; attending debates on a local council issue helped make sense of everyday politics; and lying in the grass under the trees writing poems gave onomatopoeia a real-life context.

## *Progressive education today*

And what of progressive education today? It can still be seen clearly in some aspects of educational policy and practice in New Zealand. To have the *New Zealand Curriculum* document (Ministry of Education, 2007), which sets out broad achievement objectives but leaves the topic choices to the classroom teacher, who can freely choose the teaching resources and activities, then design the assessments to suit, is very much in the progressive mould. Encouraging students to undertake inquiries of their own choosing, to work cooperatively, to participate in education outside the classroom or to engage in the creative arts are also progressive education legacies. Progressive educators would claim that children and young people who have a good sense of self-worth, a joy of discovery, a belief in fair play, who are curious, empathetic, creative, independent, co-operative, and successful will have engaged in a range of experiences from the progressive legacy that has helped shape these dispositions.

Nowhere is a progressive legacy more evident than in the early childhood curriculum. *Te Whāriki* (Ministry of Education, 1996), an innovative, holistic and integrated early childhood curriculum, views learning as a woven mat. This metaphor works at several levels. At a national level, it represents all the early childhood services as a coherent whole and, in particular, acknowledges the place of Māori culture and language in New Zealand society. At the curriculum level, it is an interlocking of the four underpinning principles (empowerment, holistic development, family and community, and relationships) and the five strands (well-being, belonging, contribution, communication, and exploration). At the level of the child, it represents the course of learning that each child will undertake—not as a linear and structured progression but as a complex interweaving of experiences and developments. *Te Whāriki* is currently under review and the results of any redevelopments will show whether the links to progressive educational philosophy have strengthened or weakened.

Despite these examples, however, progressive education is still a contested space. As with earlier critiques, progressive education has been held responsible for everything that is both good and bad about current teaching and learning. Progressive education came under attack in the 1980s from market-led ideologies that surfaced in response to economic downturn. Two ideological perspectives to impact strongly on educational decision making were neo-conservatism and neo-liberalism. Neo-conservatism aims to uphold traditional family and moral values, it supports law and order, hierarchical structures, and strong government. It values tradition, excellence, and standards. In education, neoconservatives favour a structured, subject-based curriculum where individual student progress is measured against standards by national examinations. Ideas of prescribed curricula, National Standards, cohort testing, school ranking, and teacher accountability emanate from a neoconservative perspective. Integrated curricula, student-centred inquiry, group work, peer assessment, overall teacher judgements and internal assessment credits do not fit well with this way of thinking.

Neoliberalism believes that decision making should be left to market forces. Services such as education and health are treated as commodities. Individuals can exercise free choice over their selection—as they would in a supermarket. If it is a good product, it will sell and make a profit; if it is not, the company will go out of business. Parents can choose to send their students to "good" schools and, eventually, "poor" schools will close—or be closed. Neoliberals value individualism, choice, efficiency, effectiveness and results. The purpose of schooling is to prepare children and young people for work, to strengthen the economy, and make the country competitive internationally. Schools should not be public institutions but run as businesses for profit. Teachers should receive performance-related pay. Hence the rise of charter schools, public–private partnerships, and for-profit early childhood centres. A philosophy such as progressive education that puts children at the centre of a holistic, experiential, creative learning model does not fit with the idea of education as a commodifiable product.

Yet, I see that there is hope. While teachers might feel that they are drowning in a sea of compliance and accountability, I am still inspired when I visit classrooms. Teachers find a balance between accountability and creativity and between expectations and experiences. Alongside the focus on literacy and numeracy standards are opportunities to learn through inquiries, individualised activities, cross-curricular themes, problem-solving approaches, creative and artistic pursuits and education outside the classroom. I see teachers who wish to make a difference for individual children or groups of children, especially those underserved by the system, and in the end, for the betterment of society.

While *Tomorrow's Schools* (Lange, 1988), took New Zealand further along the neoliberal path than any other countries at the time with self-managing schools, the education sector has been able to resist some of the trends that have overtaken other systems. There is a variety of pathways available through the state-funded schooling system (which accounts for 96% of schools) to cater for a range of preferences, interests, and philosophies. Teachers are still respected professionals. In 2015, 75% of respondents in a survey said teachers inspired trust and confidence (Research New Zealand, 2015). Young children in early childhood education are still encouraged to play and explore, and their learning is assessed through written and photographic narratives. There is no mandatory national testing at primary school level. National Standards can be assessed in a range of ways and teachers are trusted to make the overall judgment. At secondary school, students still get a core curriculum at Years 9 and 10 with a range of options to introduce them to a broader base of subject matter. The National Certificate of Education (NCEA) enables students to build a portfolio of credits through internal and external assessments. The choice of subjects that can be taken is wide and flexible when compared to other school systems. NCEA is the very antithesis of the kind of elitist curriculum promoted by neoconservatives.

While there are many critics—and, of course, improvements that could be made—the progressive legacy, alongside its liberal counterpart, has produced an accessible, well-rounded and relevant schooling system. It is a system that has been honed and hard-won over many years. It is important that New Zealand educators understand the genesis of the system we have today and appreciate the values that underpin our unique approach. If we wish to preserve those values into the future then we need to view education, as Dewey did, as a moral and ethical act. We also need to counter those who would change the system to its detriment. To do this requires us to view teaching as a political act (Friere, 1968) that calls us to action when those values are under threat.

## *References*

Abbiss, J. (1998). The "New Education Fellowship" in New Zealand: Its activity and influence in the 1930s and 1940s. *New Zealand Journal of Educational Studies, 33*(1), 81–93.

Alcorn, N. (1999). *To the fullest extent of his powers: C. E. Beeby's life in education*. Wellington: Victoria University Press.

Ashton-Warner, S. (1963/1886). *Teacher*. New York, NY: Simon & Shuster.

Cumming, I., & Cumming, A. (1978). *History of state education in New Zealand 1840–1975*. Carlton, VIC: Pitman Publishing.

Dewey, J. (1899). *The school and society*. Chicago, IL: University of Chicago Press.

Dewey, J. (1938). *Experience and education*. New York, NY: Collier Books.

Evers, W. (1998). How progressive education gets it wrong. *Hoover Digest, 4*. Retrieved from http://www.hoover.org/publications/hoover-digest/article/6408

Friere, P. (1968). *Pedagogy of the oppressed*. New York, NY: Seabury Press.

Lange, D. (1988). *Tomorrow's schools: The reform of education administration in New Zealand*. Wellington: Government Printer.

MacDonald, M. (2016). *Elwyn Richardson and the early world of creative education in New Zealand*. Wellington: NZCER Press

May, H. (2011). *I am five and I go to school. Early years schooling in New Zealand, 1900–2010*. Dunedin: Otago University Press.

Ministry of Education. (1996). *Te Whāriki: He whāriki mātauranga mō ngā mokopuna o Aotearoa: Early childhood curriculum*. Wellington: Learning Media.

Ministry of Education. (2007). *The New Zealand curriculum*. Wellington: Learning Media.

Neill, A. S. (1962). *Summerhill*. Harmondsworth, UK: Pelican.

Ozmon, H. (1965). Progressive education: and some of its critics. *Peabody Journal of Education, 43*(3), 169–174.

Reedy, J. (n.d.). The failure of progressive education to return to classical models. Retrieved from https://www.macalester.edu/~reedy/Samos07-ULTIssima-3[1].pdf

Research New Zealand (2015). *Trust and confidence poll*. Retrieved from http://www.researchnz.com/pdf/Research%20New%20Zealand%20-%20Trust%20and%20confidence.pdf

Richardson, E. (1964). *In the early world*. Wellington: New Zealand Council for Educational Research.

Rousseau, J.-J. (1762/1914). *Emile, or on education*. London, UK: J. M. Dent & Sons.

Wollstonecraft, M. (1792). *A vindication of the rights of woman: With strictures on political and moral subjects*. Boston, MA: Peter Edes.

THINKING ABOUT PROGRESSIVISM
IN TODAY'S WORLD

## Chapter 3 Weaving our whāriki: Re-imagining progressive philosophy in Aotearoa New Zealand early childhood education

Jacoba Matapo

*School of Critical Studies in Education*
*Faculty of Education and Social Work*
*The University of Auckland*

John Roder

*School of Learning, Development and Professional Practice*
*Faculty of Education and Social Work*
*The University of Auckland*

**Abstract**

This chapter will investigate key tenets of progressive education and identify the movement of historical events and philosophy that have influenced the context of early childhood education (ECE) in Aotearoa New Zealand. The weaving metaphor of *Te Whāriki* (Ministry of Education, 1996, 2017), our first Aotearoa New Zealand

ECE bicultural curriculum, will be explored as a cartographic method (Beradi, 2008) to analyse progressive education and provide further provocations in re-conceptualising progressive tenets in an emergent curriculum approach. Dewey's philosophy of embodied knowing and pragmatic thought will be discussed in relation to its influence on the emergent early childhood curriculum in Aotearoa New Zealand.

**Key words**

Progressivism—early childhood education—*Te Whāriki*—curriculum—kaupapa Māori

## *Introduction*

Multiple traditions are evident in the early childhood curriculum. One of these traditions is the progressive tradition, and another—which is unique to New Zealand—is a Te Ao Māori world-view. The progressive tradition within the New Zealand early childhood education (ECE) curriculum has had a lasting influence upon early childhood philosophy and pedagogy. The first early childhood curriculum, *Te Whāriki* (Ministry of Education, 1996) conceptualises learning through experience and engagement in ideals of liberal democracy, and under the guise of neoliberal free choice (Gould & Matapo, 2016). At the heart of progressive education is the rejection of the mind–body dualism, the elevation of experience, and the bridging of theory to practice. In this sense, Te Ao Māori supports that project. As explained by Mutch (2013), the "key tenets of progressive education in New Zealand are child-centeredness, experiential learning, an emergent curriculum, a holistic pedagogy and the fostering of creativity" (p. 99). Our intention for this chapter is to engage in a renewed and re-imagined philosophy of Dewey meeting *Te Whāriki* (Ministry of Education, 1996, 2017).

Here we recognise that progressive education itself is undergoing constant change through a pedagogy of democratic practices respecting experimentation, creativity, emergence, and potentiality. In what follows, we will see many traces of the traditional tenets of progressive education while explaining potentiality for reconceptualising and re-imagining. We will draw upon post-foundational philosophy, concepts of kaupapa Māori, and the metaphor of weaving that underpins our early childhood curriculum, *Te Whāriki*. We call upon the work of

Dewey, and the tenets of progressive education, experiential learning, and processual movement, tying together the weaving (a materiality of progressive education) and our emphasis in *pragmatic education*. This is not in itself novel, but follows in the tradition of the reconceptualist movement, attributed to Pinar (1995), where there has been a specific investment in reconceptualising notions of curriculum. This has influenced a targeted reconceptualisation movement in ECE, known as Reconceptualising Early Childhood Education (Bloch, 2013). In this chapter, we join with the above in an attempt to re-imagine and push past progressive education in ECE as we know it.

### Weaving te whāriki

*My hands grasping flax, harakeke*
*The movement of weaving, present–past a folding of time and space,*
*Our hands, sensing threads our bodies knowing*
*A child, mokopuna, a reflection of tūpuna in body, mind and spirit*
*And the fibres of flax, entangled with forces and flows, histories and life.*

*JM*

## Entangled histories of progressive education in Aotearoa New Zealand

Let's begin with the entangled forces and flows, the historical and political landscape of education in Aotearoa New Zealand. In what way was progressive education a reactive response to the initial efforts aimed at establishing systems of education in New Zealand? We understand it begins with the introduction of missionary-led education into New Zealand as a newly established colony of Great Britain. The early vision for education was to assimilate Māori into a new colony as a form of social control to reflect dominant English social traits (Mackey, 1967; Mutch, 2013). The 1847 Native Schools Act provided vocational training for Māori and was founded upon British industrial models of education. The disjuncture here is that the British believed such industrial models of education were more conducive to economic productivity, citizenship, and the making of a new society. The impact of this was that Māori knowledge systems of learning were dismissed. The original organisation of schools was often led by church establishments or philanthropic individuals. The first school syllabus was developed by the first Inspector-General of Schools, Reverend Habens, following the Education Act of 1877. The emphasis on the basics of the 3Rs kept some alignment with existing industrial models of education, but there were also moves towards a broader-based curriculum influenced by progressive educational theories that had, by then, permeated education philosophy (Openshaw, Lee, & Lee, 1993). This included the introduction of the arts and sciences into the curriculum (Mutch, 2013).

The history of progressive education in Aotearoa New Zealand also directly links to key events in political, social, and economic changes; these were the Great Depression of the 1930s and the New Education Fellowship (NEF) Conference of 1937 (Mutch, 2013). Progressive education was given great impetus when participants in the NEF sought to provide the New Zealand teaching profession and the public with insights into education that targeted reorganisation of education in democratic societies (Couch, 2011). As a result of this conference, organised by Clarence Beeby (the then Director of Education), the public and professional teaching bodies demanded change in New Zealand education, challenging traditional methods of pedagogy and curriculum. While the NEF Conference brought to light the need for reform in public education, the first kindergarten in New Zealand (opened in 1889) had already demonstrated strong evidence of child-centred approaches, which were informed by an egalitarian and liberal-progressive philosophy (Mutch, 2013). Key philosophers who influenced the development of early progressive ideals in ECE in New Zealand included Locke, Rousseau, and Froebel, all of whom advocated experience-based learning (see Chapter 2 in this volume for further detail). This early history of holistic and child-centred approaches left a legacy in Aotearoa New Zealand ECE that May (1997) and others believe later led to the development of *Te Whāriki*.

## Looking deeper into ECE in Aotearoa New Zealand

The context of early childhood education in Aotearoa New Zealand traverses varying factions, histories, and theories, all of which continue to influence the politics of education, and many of which are constraining, even oppressing. We work through these tensions here to show the connection and shifts in progressive education and the need for advocacy and children's rights. Over time, these have included conservative movements to preserve traditional values; liberal-left foregrounding education as a site to achieve democracy and equality; and more recently the neoliberal influence, where the libertarian right emphasises individualism, diversity, competition, and privatisation in a free-market setting (Middleton & May, 1997). The complexity of various social justice movements continues today and includes ongoing political movements promoting Māori rights and emancipation, critical feminism, and gender equality.

We could also consider here the work of reconceptualising movements promoted by educators advocating for alternative visions of ECE as political advocacy. It is vital to distinguish the history and place of ECE in Aotearoa New Zealand from histories of schooling and the compulsory sector. May (2013) claims the history of early childhood education is entangled with the histories of women's activism. Moreover, the history of early childhood education is intricately connected with social and moral agendas of the time, such as the place of women in society (Duhn, 2009). Similarly, progressive education developed as a political and ideological response to conditions of its time. It is necessary to understand its momentum as a response to contemporary conditions and understanding and insights in philosophy.

We recognise that advocacy was a key driver in the establishment of kindergartens in Aotearoa New Zealand. However, there was more to it than advocacy in response to social issues and conditions—it was also about philosophical ideas. More specifically, it was the philosophy of Froebel that underpinned the early history of kindergarten in Aotearoa New Zealand and, for the first time, the ideal of self-activity was articulated in a philosophy of play (May, 1997).

The link with progressive education is clearly evident in the democratic values of freedom, inquiry, and self-expression. These tenets can be found in John Dewey's extensive works on education philosophy. At the core is his pragmatic approach to education. Dewey's practical vision for education argued for freedom of movement, exploration, experimentation and application (Dewey, 1916). Within the compulsory sector of Aotearoa New Zealand education, Dewey's thinking was also an influence on educators such as Sylvia Ashton-Warner and Elwyn Richardson who were pushing the boundaries of the progressive tradition in their resistance to regulatory, technicist, and instrumental discourses of the time.

In recent times, there have been a number of calls in ECE research and literature to reflect more post-foundational perspectives on philosophy and practice. The call for a post-foundational stance is a direct response to the dominant discourses which favour developmentally appropriate practices that stem from foundationalism (that is, accepting universal justifications of knowledge based upon foundational beliefs). Indeed, Farquhar and White (2014) suggest the time is right for more varied paradigms and philosophical orientations that are more inclusive of a progressive education philosophy. They argue for more attention to ontologies leaning towards *pedagogy as relationship*, that is, a set of relations, "rather than [as] a response or an intervention" (p. 821). They draw on a collection of scholars who critique the current landscape as bound up in evidence-based approaches largely used "to determine 'quality early childhood education' on the basis of achieved learning outcomes." (p. 824).

A similar call has been made by the editors of the series "Contesting Early Childhood" who suggest, "a story such as that of democracy, experimentation and potentiality [also] views the world from the position of what might be termed a paradigm of post-foundationalism" (Moss, Dahlberg, Marriet Olsson, & Vandenbroeck, 2016, p. 7). These authors, many of whom have ties with the reconceptualists, go on to suggest that, rather than seeking "certainty, control and objectivity, the post-foundationalist welcomes and seeks to work with complexity, uncertainty and unpredictability" (2016, p. 7). Echoing this call, we avoid any central foundational unity and adopt post-structural perspectives in our discussion, such that consideration is given to the complexity and the multiplicity of relations that are opened up through a rich sensory, experiential engagement with the world.

## Dewey and pragmatic thought in education— our hands, sensing threads our bodies knowing …

How does Dewey's educational project push us to look beyond the dominance of intellectual abstract rational thought? In response to this question, we now lead into Dewey's pragmatic philosophy of education; his advocacy for sensory and experiential engagement with the world and learning as life produced through richer connections and relations arising through experience. Indeed, learning and life, in Deweyan terms, are inseparable. Dewey's naturalistic and organic model of experience places the individual along with the environment in a constant reciprocally transactional relationship, whereby each transforms the other. This transaction manifests as experience (Dewey, 1916). For Dewey, experimental logic and the process of inquiry requires specific conditions: where there is freedom in thinking and learning, where intellectual initiative is exercised, and where individual variations allow for intellectual freedom. Dewey's theories responded to the constraints of tightly prescribed, outcome-focused education. For Dewey, it was about experiential learning in all its various forms: experimental inquiry, naturalistic inquiry, and inquiry into inquiry. He sought a transformation to more educative and process-oriented practices. In contrast to an education based on abstract ideals and universals of foundational theories, it is in the focus on the link between disciplined inquiry and experience in which Dewey located his pragmatic vision of education. Inquiry as an active process "does not live in an environment; it lives by means of an environment … and with differentiation of structure the environment expands" (Dewey, 1938, p. 25).

As indicated earlier, the philosophy of Froebel influenced early progressive ideals in ECE, and in the essence of Froebel's work, Dewey sought to clarify his views of learning and play when he published *Froebel's Educational Principles* (Dewey, 1915). Dewey came to emphasise the importance of the social context of learning, rejecting American psychologist Granville Stanley Hall's evolutionary views of development (May, 1997). Dewey's educational theory emphasises problem solving and co-operation, whereas the education context promotes a community of learners engaged in the reconstruction of experience. As May (1997) notes, "Dewey came to see that educational theory was about adjustment and adaptation to the social environment" (p. 112). Dewey's view of activity and play were at the core of his wider views on the function of education in relation to society. The grounding of play in the child's experiences of the real world is not identified by Dewey as anything a child does externally, rather Dewey (1915) argues that play designates a child's mental attitude in its entirety:

> It is the free play, the interplay, of all the child's powers, thoughts, and physical movements in embodying, in a satisfying form, his own images and interests ... it means that the supreme end of the child is fullness of growth—fullness of realization of his building of powers, a realization which continually carries him on from one place to another. (p. 73)

Unlike a society based upon tradition where uniformity or sameness is the leading ideal, a progressive society values individual variations as a means for growth. In a democratic society, there must be an allowance for intellectual freedom (Dewey, 1916). So, where to push the pragmatist boundaries upon which Dewey originally located his educational, philosophical legacy? We intend an ontology of affective relations, not only as Dewey would argue for (relation with nature and people), but with pedagogy seen as relationship, valuing multiplicities, complexity, and uncertainty. We believe this invites a shift to a post-foundational analysis and direction; one we think might be worthy of further exploration and experimentation.

We noted earlier that cartography (Beradi, 2008) has been employed in mapping the set of conceptual/social/historical/material relations both followed and generated in the writing thus far. We will now extend the traditional conceptions of pragmatism and suggest an ontological position that contests the Cartesian mind–body dualism (that the mind operates in separation to the body) and explore what a body can do (in all its collective, social, historical, visible material and invisible, immaterial relations). Like Semetsky (another author who has reconceptualised the philosophy of Dewey), we believe that seeking such a re-imagining is in line with Dewey's project—urging both open-mindednesses and rejection of fixedness. It is in the spirit of Deweyan philosophy that we argue for progressive education to remain open to an ongoing commitment to transformation through reflection that takes account of the changing contexts in which it occurs.

> If in this process Deweyan thought itself undergoes changes and reorganization, it only confirms, as Jim Garrison (1995) has indicated, that Dewey himself, in accord with his philosophical project, would welcome the reconstruction of his own ideas so as "to better respond to the vicissitudes of new times and contexts." (Garrison, 1995, p. 1, as cited in Semetsky, 2006)

Re-imagining curriculum that takes account of *affect* would extend progressive education beyond human-centric, child-centred practices to an emergent and relational space, open to affecting and being affected by all bodies within the assemblage—social, corporeal, and non-corporeal. This is where we look now to see potentiality within a bicultural kaupapa that signals beliefs and practices beyond the individualistic paradigms of Western human-subjectivity and weaves together alternate trajectories. We ask how alternate trajectories are produced in the weaving our whāriki.

## *Weaving our whāriki: An emergent, holistic curriculum*

The weaving of the first Aotearoa New Zealand early childhood curriculum draft of *Te Whāriki* was initiated in 1993. The final version was released in 1996. It was not until 2016 that the review of *Te Whāriki* was initiated. This means that, for 20 years, the early childhood curriculum document remained unchanged. Through this period, the curriculum gained international interest and has remained highly regarded globally (Ministry of Education, 2016). The history of this document is testament to the persistence of leaders, teachers, and academics who sought to strengthen the profession of early childhood education. They also ensured extensive consultation (sector-wide) to be inclusive of all diverse ECE services. *Te Whāriki* is a metaphor to demonstrate the collective weaving of peoples, principles, and strands. It is designed to engage both Māori and non-Māori epistemologies. Another dimension of *Te Whāriki* is the creative nexus of weaving; this embodied processual constituent is open to new and emerging relations—it is kept in movement.

Although the 1996 version of *Te Whāriki* draws upon key Western theories including Vygotsky's sociocultural theory (Vygotsky, 1962), Piagetian cognitive constructivist theory (Piaget, 1959), and Bronfenbrenner's ecological model (Bronfenbrenner, 1974), the kaupapa for *Te Whāriki* suggests other ways of knowing and coming to know. The precolonial Māori image of the child is of entangled histories, spirituality, and materiality located with whenua (land) and geographical ties to places (one's tūrangawaewae). Whenua is the term used for placenta, afterbirth, and land. Consequently, land has as profound a significance as the placenta which surrounds the embryo. The whenua provides "warmth and security, a mauri, a life force that relates to and interacts with Mother earth's forces" (Jenkins & Harte, 2011, p. 8).

The notion of the individual child is challenged through a Māori indigenous perspective, as the child is located only within the collective (this includes relations with animate and inanimate objects). The early education of Māori children was situated within the collective—the whānau, iwi, and hapu—where children contributed to daily tasks and decision-making. As Reedy (2013) has suggested, "the child was, and still is, the incarnation of the ancestors … the living link with yesterday … the binding rope that ties people together … and the embodiment of the aspirations of tomorrow" (p. 40).

Why is it important to understand the indigenous Māori image of the child? The resurgence of Māori kaupapa in Māori political movements that later informed our first bicultural curriculum situates the Māori child as mokopuna (an image of tūpuna, in body, mind, and spirit). This is inclusive of spiritual dimensions, genealogy, and geographical ties, as well as material relations. The bicultural nature of *Te Whāriki* has been contested by a number of scholars who have identified implications in praxis due to the political and social factors influencing early childhood contexts and teachers in a free-market climate (Gould & Matapo, 2016; Rau & Ritchie, 2011; Tesar, 2015).

As a curriculum framework, bringing together values, pedagogical practices and theory, *Te Whāriki* has, for over 20 years, remained relevant to the many early childhood contexts in which it has been implemented. The strength of *Te Whāriki* lies in the holistic approach to curriculum and the openness of the curriculum to adaptation at local levels. Osberg and Biesta (2008) argue for the logic of emergence in education; however, they identify the contradictions for educators in meanings that emerge that are incompatible with the aims of education. Dahlberg, Moss, and Pence (2013) warn of the dangers of tightly defined frameworks and the limitations of such frameworks leading towards rigidity and irrelevance to local situations, which risk being disregarded. As curriculum frameworks are socially constructed and are normative representations, they are value-laden and can be problematic for teachers in keeping open a vision for education (Dahlberg, Moss, & Pence, 2013).

The idea of an emergent curriculum is often associated with *Te Whāriki*. The concept of emergence stems from pragmatist, creative constructivist, post-structuralist, and *emergentist* epistemologies and is linked to complexity theory. Within such paradigms, knowledge is not reducible to the representation of the real; rather, knowledge can be understood to emerge in our participation in the world (Osberg & Biesta, 2008). This understanding of *emergence of meaning* raises the question of what kinds of meaning(s) are allowed to emerge in the ECE context and to what extent pre-determined learning outcomes limit the formation of new subjectivities (Sellers, 2010, 2013). Osberg and Biesta (2008) argue that the purpose of education has become to shape the subjectivity of the students, with the primary purpose of promoting specific outcomes that are deemed important. Dahlberg and Moss (2005) invite early childhood teachers to critique widely accepted dominant discourses such as self-regulating, constructivist pedagogy and theory.

The underpinning aspiration of *Te Whāriki* is that children grow up as "competent and confident learners and communicators, healthy in mind, body and spirit, secure in their sense of belonging and in the knowledge that they make a valued contribution to society" (Ministry of Education, 2017, p. 6). From this statement, it could be argued that the aim of education is to produce responsible citizens. The *competent, autonomous and flexible child* is prevalent in traditional forms of constructivism. This subjectivity of the empowered child who problem solves, analyses, and reflects is created to fit the neoliberal workforce, as well as fostering liberalists' ideals of citizenship (Gould & Matapo, 2016). According to Dahlberg (2003), within contemporary society, conceptions of competent and autonomous behaviour have become another way of governing subjects. What this aspiration statement lacks is consideration of *otherness* and *difference* that are affirmed within a post-structuralist and emergentist epistemology. Curricula, as Dahlberg et al. (2013) explain,

> … can readily become normative, deadening innovation and aspiration … More generally, they can lead to a false sense of security,

by seeming to offer certainties and guarantees ... Let us recognise their limitations and dangers, their assumptions and values. Let them not be at the expense of ignoring other ways of thinking about and making sense of early childhood institutions and the work that they do. (pp. 122–123)

## Re-imagining progressive education in early childhood

Like the ontology of pragmatic thought, the embodied metaphor of weaving orientates towards connections, is open to relations, and is open to difference and respect for difference, being non-prescriptive. We, as teachers and the wider ECE sector, are part of the weaving, the processual movement, the making and remaking of curriculum. We have challenged acquired meaning by way of emergentist epistemologies. As Osberg and Biesta (2008) explain, in an emergentist epistemology "... meaning is continuously made and remade through engagement with our world ... meaning therefore, is not something one can ever have" (p. 325). When applying an ontology of emergence, relational pedagogy must be concerned with the responsibility in which human-subjectivity comes into being. Education, we believe, must be re-imagined, not in a spirit of mediocre reformist rethinking, but in the spirit of an ontology of emergence. What we have tried to suggest here is a space opening to further transformation of the progressive trajectory, whilst still being one of advocacy and experiential dimensions, it now makes a significant ontological shift.

### Weaving te whāriki

*My hands grasping flax, harakeke*
*The movement of weaving, present-past a folding of time and space,*
*Our hands, sensing threads our bodies knowing*
*A child, mokopuna a reflection of tūpuna in body, mind and spirit*
*And the fibres of flax, entangled with forces and flows, histories and life*
*How do we weave present-past and future, a whāriki for wisdom, for a people yet to come?*

*JM.*

## References

Beradi, F. (2008). *Félix Guattari: Thought, friendship, and visionary cartography* (G. Mecchia & C. J. Stivale, Eds. & Trans.). Basingstoke, UK: Palgrave Macmillan.

Bloch, M. N. (2013). Reconceptualising theory/policy/curriculum/pedagogy in early child (care and) education: Reconceptualizing early childhood (RECE) 1991–2012. *International Journal of Equity and Innovation in Early Childhood, 11*(1), 65–85.

Bronfenbrenner, U. (1979). *The ecology of human development.* Cambridge, MA: Harvard University Press.

Couch, D. (2011). *New Zealand education's progressive origin: 1937 to 1944: The seven years from idea to orthodoxy.* Unpublished master's thesis, The University of Auckland.

Dahlberg, G. (2003). Pedagogy as a loci of an ethics of an encounter. In M. Bloch, K. Holmund, I. Moqvist, & T. Popkewitz (Eds.), *Governing children, families and education. Restructuring the welfare state* (pp. 261–286). New York, NY: Palgrave Macmillan.

Dahlberg, G., & Moss, P. (2005). *Ethics and politics in early childhood education.* Oxford, UK: RoutledgeFalmer.

Dahlberg, G., Moss, P., & Pence, A. (2013). *Beyond quality in early childhood education and care, languages of evaluation.* London, UK: Routledge.

Dewey, J. (1915). *The school and society.* Chicago, IL: University of Chicago Press.

Dewey, J. (1916). *Democracy and education: An introduction to the philosophy of education.* New York, NY: Macmillan.

Dewey, J. (1938). *Logic: The theory of inquiry.* New York, NY: Holt.

Duhn, I. (2009). Early childhood education. In E. Rata & R. Sullivan (Eds.), *Introduction to the history of New Zealand education* (pp. 31–43). Auckland: Pearson.

Farquhar, S., & White, E. J. (2014). Philosophy and pedagogy of early childhood. *Educational Philosophy and Theory, 46*(8), 821–832. doi:10.1080/00131857.2013.783964

Garrison, J. W. (1995). *The new scholarship on Dewey.* Dordrecht, The Netherlands: Kluwer Academic.

Gould, K., & Matapo, J. (2016). What's in a philosophy statement? A critical discourse analysis of early childhood centre philosophy statements in Aotearoa/New Zealand. *He Kupu, 4*(3), 51–60.

Jenkins, K., & Harte, H. M. (2011). *Traditional Māori parenting: A historical review of literature of traditional Māori child rearing practices in pre-European times.* Auckland: Te Kahui Mana Ririki.

Mackey, J. (1967). *The making of a state education system: The passing of the New Zealand Education Act 1877.* London, UK: Geoffrey Chapman.

May, H. (2013). *The discovery of early childhood* (2nd ed). Wellington: NZCER Press.

Middleton, S., & May, H. (1997). *Teachers talk teaching 1915–1995: Early childhood, schools and teachers' colleges.* Palmerston North: Dunmore Press.

Ministry of Education. (1996). *Te whāriki: He whāriki mātauranga mo ngā mokopuna o Aotearoa: Early childhood curriculum.* Wellington: Learning Media.

Ministry of Education. (2016). *Te whāriki: He whāriki mātauranga mo ngā mokopuna o Aotearoa: Early childhood curriculum, draft for consultation.* Wellington: Learning Media.

Ministry of Education. (2017). *Te whāriki: He whāriki mātauranga mo ngā mokopuna o Aotearoa. Early childhood curriculum. Draft for consultation.* Wellington, Learning Media.

Moss, P., Dahlberg, G., Marriet Olsson, L., & Vandenbroeck, M. (2016). *Why contest early childhood?* "Contesting Early Childhood series", 14. Retrieved from https://www.routledge.com/education/posts/10150?utm_source=shared_link&utm_medium=post&utm_campaign=160701429

Mutch, C. (2013). Progressive education in New Zealand: A revered past, a contested present and an uncertain future. *International Journal of Progressive Education, 9*(2), 98–116.

Openshaw, R., Lee, L., & Lee, H. (1993). *Challenging the myths: Rethinking New Zealand's educational history.* Palmerston North: Dunmore Press.

Osberg, D., & Biesta, G. (2008). The emergent curriculum: Navigating a complex course between unguided learning and planned enculturation. *Journal of Curriculum Studies, 40*(3), 313–328.

Piaget, J. (1959). *The language and thought of the child* (3rd ed.). New York, NY: Routledge and Kegan Paul.

Pinar, W. (1995). *Understanding curriculum: An introduction to the study of historical and contemporary curriculum discourses.* New York, NY: Peter Lang Publishing.

Rau, C., & Ritchie, J. (2011). Aha koa he iti: Early childhood pedagogies affirming of Māori children's rights to their culture. *Early Education and Development, 22*(5), 795–847.

Reedy, T. (2013). Tōku rangitiratanga nā te mana mātauranga: "Knowledge and power set me free." In J. Nuttall (Ed,), *Weaving Te Whāriki* (2nd ed). Wellington: NZCER Press.

Sellers, M. (2010). Re(con)ceiving young children's curricular performativity. *International Journal of Qualitative Studies in Education, 23*(5), 557–577.

Sellers, M. (2013). *Young children becoming curriculum: Deleuze, Te Whāriki and curricular understandings.* London, UK: Routledge.

Semetsky, I. (2006). *Deleuze, education and becoming.* Rotterdam, The Netherlands: Sense Publishers.

Tesar. M. (2015). Te Whāriki in Aotearoa/New Zealand. Witnessing and resisting neo-liberal and neo-colonial discourses in early childhood education. In V. Pacini Ketchabaw & A. Taylor (Eds.), *Unsettling colonial places and spaces* (pp. 145–170). London, UK: Routledge.

Vygotsky, L. S. (1962). *Thought and language.* Cambridge MA: MIT Press.

## Progressivism Discussion starters

1. What aspects of progressive education are still prevalent in today's classrooms and early childhood centres? Why do you think these aspects have endured? How have these aspects evolved or been adapted?
2. What aspects of progressive education appear to be in conflict with some of today's education policies? How do schools/centres and teachers attempt to resolve these tensions?
3. What critiques of progressive ideals are made by the media, general public, or politicians? Why have these aspects come under scrutiny? How valid do you think this scrutiny is? What improvements might you suggest?
4. Dewey is mentioned by many of the writers in this book. What is it about Dewey's ideas that mean they still resonate today? How do Dewey's ideas help us make sense of some of today's educational issues?

TRADITION 2: LIBERALISM

# Liberalism—a personal reflection

Maria Perreau

*School of Critical Studies in Education*
*Faculty of Education and Social Work*
*The University of Auckland*

## Introduction
Reflecting on a decade of being in the classroom, the author presents some experiences of contrasting approaches to teaching and learning in schools she has worked in. She compares an instrumental, content-based, and assessment-driven approach with a liberal concept-based approach. Through her own education journey, she has come to know the liberating and transformative power of knowledge and the joy of a love of learning.

## The transformative power of knowledge
I grew up in a small Hawke's Bay town, close to a large extended family who worked hard in fairly working-class jobs. Neither of my parents completed 5 years of high school—neither was given the opportunity to do so. Dad left school at 15 to earn money to contribute to his family, then joined the army. He could read and write and calculate;

that was enough for him. Mum was told by the nuns at school that she was not university material (so few girls were) and my grandfather arranged for her to learn book-keeping with his accountant's office. She was never asked what she would rather do. By the time I was in school, my parents had set up their own business growing hydroponic tomatoes in large, plastic greenhouses. It was a hard way to make a living but we had plenty of fresh produce and certainly never went hungry. However, my parents aspired to more for their children. Education, learning, and knowledge were a big focus in our house simply because my parents were determined to give their three daughters the opportunities that were not on offer to them due to their life circumstances. We had choices; there were no limits to our dreams if we studied hard and worked hard. And so, we did. The Perreau girls, as we were known collectively, became the first university graduates in my father's family.

I knew exactly what I wanted to do with my degree: become an English, history, and social studies teacher. I wanted to introduce new generations to the power of language and articulation, to critical thinking and the analysis of texts, understanding what it is to be human and what it is to be a member of society. I wanted to spark curiosity and develop inquiring minds. And so, I became a teacher. However, as a secondary teacher, teaching senior students, I quickly became caught up in the all-consuming focus of assessments. Reflecting back now, I realise that I was influenced by the culture of the school instead of prioritising teaching for knowledge and conceptual understanding. My lessons approached learning with an attitude of "this is what you will be assessed on, so this is what we need to focus on". My job became getting students to pass assessments. It felt like that was all that mattered. The learning was not promoted for its intrinsic value, but rather as a means to an end. I was fulfilling an expected role in that particular school culture. I did it very well, and my students passed their assessments and entered university.

A few years later I began teaching in a dedicated middle school (not in New Zealand), and taught only students from years 7 to 9. I quickly noticed the difference in approach to the learning that we as a teaching team were facilitating for our students. My 3 years' teaching at this middle school were rich in learning experiences for me as an educator. As I reflect back on this experience, I can say that the culture of the school strongly reflected the values of a liberal education. We put knowledge at the heart of learning inquiries and asked: "What is it that we want the students to know?" Our decisions, as professionals, were centred around teaching for conceptual understandings deemed important by our knowledge of our disciplines. I taught English and drama, and met with the social studies, maths, science, art, music, and PE teachers regularly to plan curricula that linked and strengthened student understandings. Over a fortnight, students had equal hours of each learning area taught in 80-minute blocks. We worked collaboratively to make connections visible and looked for ways to help students see that knowledge is transferable from a particular inquiry and applicable to new contexts, other situations. Of course, we assessed the students, but we developed assessments *for* learning as well as *of* learning. We had a lot of fun, and the high academic expectations we fostered challenged the students to learn without burdening them with pressure about how they'd have to do well in assessments to have a good life.

What I learnt in those years is that there is a real difference between an approach to learning that places knowledge at the forefront for its own intrinsic value and an approach that uses knowledge as something to learn to pass a standard, or to help boost the statistics of achievement of a school on an ERO report. One of the things that stands out to me the most is the attitude that students have towards learning when it is framed as being of value in its own right. Compare, for example, the following statements that could be used to introduce a new unit of inquiry:

1. For the next 8 weeks, we will explore the concept of power. What is power? How is it gained? How is it maintained? These are the essential questions that you'll be able to answer by the end of this unit.

2. Our next unit is a novel study. We'll be reading *Animal Farm* by George Orwell. You will be assessed on your ability to write an essay showing that you understand the concept of power and how it is gained and maintained.

Over the years, I have used both of these types of statements and neither is right or wrong; however, in my experience, leading with an inquiry question framing the learning as a search for knowledge—about the nature of power in this case—stimulates curiosity and engagement.

Then, after a few lessons, I would introduce the assessment to students and frame it in a way that highlights this as an opportunity to show their understanding of the concept as well as develop valuable, transferrable skills—communicating ideas clearly, structuring an argument coherently, using evidence to back up claims and interpretations, and so on. The assessment becomes an integral part of the learning, but it is not framed as the *reason* for the learning. It is well worth noting that this liberal approach invigorated and inspired me as a teacher as well.

In my educational journey, I cannot help but wonder what my father and mother would have chosen for themselves if they had had an education like mine. If Mum had been born a generation later, for example, she may well be an accountant, not an assistant to one. And Dad, if he'd been able to remain in school, what knowledge pathway would he have pursued? Well, he did return to education and graduated with his Bachelor of Computing Systems when he was in his 50s. Neither of my parents have regrets about the lives they have led but they both agree that it would have been great to have had the opportunities to make more choices for themselves when they were younger. I am grateful that I have chosen a career that empowers the next generations of young people to do just that.

LIBERALISM—HISTORY AND CONCEPTS

# Chapter 4  Daring to know: The liberal tradition and education

## Alexis Siteine

*School of Critical Studies in Education*
*Faculty of Education and Social Work*
*The University of Auckland*

**Abstract**

This chapter argues that ideas such as individual freedom, stemming from the time of the Enlightenment, continue to influence current educational thought and practice. The chapter outlines the development of liberal thought and discusses the three main principles of a liberal education: commitment to the individual; the ideal of equal opportunity; and the role of knowledge and rationality. An argument is made for the centrality of moving learners beyond their own experience into the challenging and complex world of powerful knowledge.

**Key words**

Liberalism—freedom—equality—powerful knowledge

## Introduction

Liberal education arises from the philosophies and politics of the Enlightenment; a time of intellectual movements in the 17th and 18th centuries when traditional beliefs were challenged by new ideas about the relationship between the individual and society. A leading Enlightenment philosopher, Immanuel Kant, captured the spirit of the times in the Enlightenment creed, "*Sapere aude!* 'Dare to know!'" and in his commitment to the ability of individuals to think for themselves (Kant, 1784/1995, p. 1).

This chapter places the public education systems of the 19th and 20th centuries within the context of ideas about individual freedom (or liberty) developed by Enlightenment thinkers in order to show how these ideas continue to influence current educational thought and practices.

A liberal education is characterised by three main principles. The first is a commitment to the individual. It recognises that individuals are different so does not claim equal outcomes (the idea behind an "equity" or equal outcomes approach) but instead emphasises the right of all children to become fully autonomous, self-determining individuals. The second principle is the ideal of equal opportunity. Despite individual differences, the liberal commitment is to providing opportunities for all children to reach their full potential. This implies the existence of a just and equitable society. The third principle concerns the role of knowledge in the individual's journey to freely take up life's opportunities. To do this a person needs to have developed the ability to think rationally, an ability that occurs only through engagement with the complex ideas of academic subjects encountered in years of schooling (Rata, 2012; Young, 2008).

The purpose of a liberal education is to benefit both the individual and society; to individualise and to socialise, in other words. Individuals are to be responsible for their own lives but they must also contribute to a society able to provide equal opportunity. It is for these reasons that liberal educators are committed to socialising children to become citizens and to providing access to what Michael Young has recently referred to as "powerful knowledge" (Young & Muller, 2013).

This liberal vision for New Zealand education is found in Peter Fraser's famous 1939 statement of "education as opportunity":

> The Government's objective, broadly expressed, is that every person, whatever his level of academic ability, whether he be rich or poor, whether he live in town or country, has a right, as a citizen, to a free education of the kind for which he is best fitted, and to the fullest extent of his powers. So far is this from being a mere pious platitude that the full acceptance of the principle will involve the reorientation of the education system. (Fraser, 1939, pp. 2–3)

The liberal mantras of "equality of opportunity" and "rights and responsibilities" were commonplace in New Zealand education until the 1980s and can be traced to the evolving shifts in liberal thinking from the Enlightenment. To demonstrate these historical influences, I identify three phases of liberalism, each with the modern ideas about individual freedom, self-determination, and access to rational knowledge at their core. That historical account also provides the context for the major part of this chapter, which is concerned with the way in which these philosophical and political ideas have influenced educational policy, curriculum, and practice. I argue that the principles of a liberal education are a valid approach to education in the 21st century, with the ideas of equality of opportunity for individuals and groups, an opportunity achieved through access to the powerful knowledge found in academic subjects still relevant to education in the 21st century.

I recently read an article about education where the author described herself as a "liberal educator." Since the 1980s, the shift from equality of opportunity to equity, and from knowledge-centred to student-centred education has seen the term "liberal education" fall into disuse. This writer's assertive self-description caused me to pause in my reading to consider not only what the writer meant about herself, but also what it means to be a liberal educator, especially in New Zealand today. Given the renewed interest in many liberal ideas about education in recent years, especially those concerning knowledge, my purpose is to use the next section to remind readers about the ideas which are core liberal values. This discussion of liberalism more generally is followed by a longer section where I discuss the ways in which these ideas have influenced education. Within this discussion, I present an argument as to why a liberal education remains a valid approach to schooling and learning in the 21st century.

## What is liberalism?

As a political philosophy, liberalism is based on the twin concepts of liberty and equality. The term "liberty" is most often used synonymously with freedom, but the concept of liberty can be differentiated from the concept of freedom. Pitkin (1988) describes liberty as one of the "fruits" or consequences of freedom (p. 524). Liberty is granted to an individual or group by a person or institution. Freedom, on the other hand, is the individual's ability to make decisions unencumbered by any external control. Importantly, the role of knowledge, and the type of knowledge which enables us to think rationally, is deeply embedded in these notions of freedom and liberty. Accordingly, Lalor (1899) describes liberalism as the "liberty to think" that is then "recognised and practiced" (p. 760). Freedoms espoused by liberals such as freedom of speech, freedom of education and religion, and civil rights "are derived from and may not exist without the freedom to think" (p. 760). This is the connection between knowledge and freedom recognised even earlier by Mary Wollstonecraft in her 1798 work *A Vindication of the Rights of Woman*. Her statement also captures another idea in liberalism—that the rights of the individual do not come without the responsibility to one's role in society: "Make women rational creatures, and free citizens, and they will quickly become good wives and mothers; that is,—if men do not neglect the duties of husbands and fathers" (p. 311). She clearly assumes the liberal concept of equality in her reference to gender roles. Equality is the idea that all people should be treated as equals on the basis of their humanity. Although this is accepted as a basic right in the modern world, it was a truly revolutionary idea in the 18th century. Indeed, both the American and French revolutions attested to the revolutionary nature of these liberal ideas. Irrespective of their social or economic status, individuals, it was claimed, should enjoy the same political, social, economic and civil rights. These notions of liberty and equality have played out in different ways throughout three broad phases of liberalism: classical liberalism, social liberalism, and neoliberalism.

*Classical liberalism*

Classical liberalism emphasises the role of liberty. The motivation for classical liberals was to overthrow the established order of state absolutism in favour of the autonomous individual. Absolutism and elitism, or in the then-popular phrase "the tyranny of tradition", had to be eradicated if individuals were to have the right to make serious decisions for themselves about how society should function. The development of self-reliant individuals and, in turn, independent communities could overcome the subordination to the state or to other forms of traditional authority that was, in the pre-Enlightenment era, a common human condition. Subordination to the state or church was possible in the absence of individual rights.

John Locke in his work *Two Treatises of Government* (1772/2002) proposes a view of governance based on concepts that are fundamental to a modern democracy. He defended the claim that people are by nature free and equal against claims that God had made all people naturally subject to a monarch. The existence of these natural rights or human rights are those rights that are universal, intrinsic to being human, and that are not within the purview of a governing body to grant or withdraw. Locke argued that rights, such as the right to life, liberty, and property, have a foundation independent of the laws of any particular society. He used the claim that individuals are naturally free and equal as part of the justification for understanding legitimate political government as the result of a social contract. In this contract, people agreed to be governed as long as government protected their rights and served their best interests (Tuckness, 2016). In addition to the promotion of natural or human rights, Thomas Hobbes, often referred to as a founder of liberalism, argued that individuals naturally pursued their own self-interests and while the role of government was to protect individual rights, government should also protect individuals from each other where conflicting self-interests existed.

*Social liberalism*

Where classical liberalism emphasises the role of liberty and universal, human, or natural rights, social liberalism stresses the importance of equality. It is similar to classical liberalism in the promotion and expansion of civil and political rights and liberties, but differs in the belief that individual liberty may require a level of social justice. Government is not limited to the Hobbesian view that its role is to protect individuals from each other. It also includes addressing economic and social issues such as poverty, health care, and education. From the perspective of social liberalism, the good of society is viewed as contributing to the freedom of the individual.

In the early 20th century, social liberal policies were implemented in many Western democracies in order to provide more equal acquisition of the "basics of a decent life". Government intervention was required to achieve this. The classical liberalism of the 18th and 19th centuries led to an increasing division between those who had prospered in times of economic growth and those who did not have the same access or opportunity. Social liberalism emerged following periods of war and economic depression where the role of the government included the provision of initiatives based on principles of equity and social justice. It reflects a belief described by Falk, Hampton, Hodgkinson, Parker, and Rorris (1993) that:

> there are some things which people should have, that there are basic needs that should be fulfilled, that burdens and rewards should not be spread too divergently across the community, and that policy should be directed with impartiality, fairness and justice towards these ends. (p. 2)

## *Neoliberalism*

The third phase of liberalism discussed in this section promotes an increased role for the economic market and a reduced role for the state when it comes to regulating society. Neoliberalism is a reaction to the increased role of state in human affairs during the phase of social liberalism since the early 20th century. This reaction did not result in a return to classical liberalism, as governments continued to provide social services and retained control over economic policy, but state intervention is viewed as less efficient than the free market in promoting economic growth and in allocating resources (Codd, 2008).

Codd (2005) describes this phase of liberalism as promoting:

> individual rights to property ownership, legal protection and market freedom, within a social environment of enterprise and competition. Each of these social constructions of the citizen has particular

implications for education policy and the role of the state in the provision of public schooling. (p. 196)

## What is a liberal education?

This section returns to the philosophical ideas of liberty and equality to discuss the way in which these concepts have influenced educational policy, curriculum, and practice in order to describe a liberal education.

### Liberty or freedom

One of the changes that accompanied the movement away from absolute rule or rule by tradition towards more democratic forms of government was the development of ideas about individual political, civil, and economic rights and the inclusion of these ideas in politics. In the 18th century, writers such as Mary Wollstonecraft saw the rational thinking acquired from being educated as the means to promote these individual rights. Thomas Jefferson went further to claim that the success of a democratic government depended on an informed public. He saw a democratic society as one comprised of educated and enlightened individuals who had the freedom to make their own choices (Ravitch, 2001). In keeping with the aim of the early liberals to limit the power of government over the individual, Jefferson hoped schools would be the instruments by which students could arm themselves with literacy and knowledge against the intrusion of the state in human affairs. Schooling thus would be the means to liberate individuals from the powers to which they had traditionally been subordinated, what Eric Fromm (1956) referred to as "the incestuous ties of clan and soil" (p. 69), and French revolutionaries as the tyranny of tradition.

What is the relevance of these various liberal ideas for education systems in countries that have enjoyed at least one century of democracy—in New Zealand's case, over a century and a half since the basic form of parliament democracy was established by the New Zealand Constitution Act of 1853? A response can be found in the answers to the proposition put by Bailey (1984). He asks, if education is to liberate then what is it that children should be liberated *from* and what are they to be liberated *for*? All children, he explains, irrespective of their social, economic, and ethnic backgrounds, "are born into specific and limited circumstances of geography, economy, social class" (p. 21). These circumstances, he argues, can either:

> entrap or confirm a young person in the limiting circumstances of his birth, or it can be of a kind that will widen his horizons, increase his awareness of choice, reveal his prejudices and superstitions as such and multiply his points of reference and comparison. (p. 21)

Education can, therefore, liberate children from, in Bailey's words, "the present and particular" of their birth. A liberal education, then, will not be confined to only that which is "localised" knowledge, "relevant" to the circumstances of the learner (Rata, 2012). Rather, it seeks to provide access to knowledge beyond the learner's immediate experience or that which they know beyond the school.

If children are to be liberated from their limiting circumstances, what are they to be liberated for? Bailey's (1984) explanation reflects the ideas of Jefferson stated above, namely that a liberal education should lead to an individual who is a free moral agent, who can exercise both intellectual and moral autonomy; in other words, someone who has the capacity to choose their own beliefs and their own actions, someone who is not a servant of the church or state, or a slave to the choices of others. John Stuart Mill described the nature of intellectual autonomy when he declared:

> He who lets the world, or his own portion of it, choose his plan of life for him, has no need of any other faculty than the ape-like one of imitation. He who chooses his plan for himself, employs all his faculties. He must use observation to see, reasoning and judgment to foresee, activity to gather materials for decision, discrimination to decide, and when he has decided, firmness and self-control to hold to his deliberate decision. (Mill, 1859/2002, p. 123)

This is what it is to be truly human. A link can be drawn between this characteristic of a liberal education and Freire's notion of humanisation. Liberation, from a Freirean point of view, consists in the struggle against oppression. This struggle, from a liberal perspective, is characterised in the development of moral autonomy and is manifest as self-government rather than imposition. Jonathan (1997) puts it this way:

> The enduring ideal of liberal philosophy of education—of the emancipation of persons from the constraints of their contingent

circumstance—becomes inseparable from a socially transformative purpose for education. (p. 207).

The extent to which an education is liberal is the extent to which it liberates rather than confirms or entraps in the conditions and structures of circumstance. (See Chapter 1 of this book for a fuller discussion of Freire's work.)

### Equality

If this is the role of liberty, then what of equality? The liberal concern with equality is expressed within education as a requirement that education can and should meet social justice ends. As an approach to education it is concerned with increasing equality of opportunities as well as equity (of access) and a particular conception of social and educational justice (Jonathan, 1997).

Different educational traditions offer a range of theories and make different claims about how education can promote equality. Sociologists of education interested in a realist approach to knowledge propose a view that aligns with a liberal education. They make the claim that disciplinary knowledge "offers important possibilities" for the promotion and achievement of social and educational justice (Barrett, 2017; Beck, 2013; Moore, 2013; Rata, 2012; Young & Muller, 2013. Barrett and Rata (2014) point out that "one of the most fundamental inequalities in education is that of access to the most powerful knowledge" (p. 1). Powerful knowledge refers to forms of knowledge that "gives power to those who have access to it" (Young, 2010, p. 11). The fundamental role of schools is to provide opportunities for students to obtain this kind of knowledge; that which is found only in academic subjects not in a student's socio-cultural experience. It is a way of promoting social and educational justice. However, this approach, which veers away from the relativist and materialist views for achieving social educational justice has made it vulnerable to accusations of elitism.

## Characteristics of a liberal education

What are the characteristics, then, of a liberal education? Several educators have attempted to identify what is it that makes a liberal education (see, for example, Crittenden, 2006; Hirst, 1972/2010; Jonathan, 1997; Nussbaum, 2004). All of these educators recognise the characteristics of liberty or freedom as significant to a liberal education. Although freedom, emancipation, or empowerment are also claimed by other approaches to education, liberal education in particular has a strong claim to these ideas in its connection to the Enlightenment writers. Liberty itself, as a characteristic of a liberal education, is "freedom from the present and particular" for the development of the self-governing, rational individual" (Bailey, 1984, p. 22). Although these words are written by a contemporary writer, they could well be those of the 18th century scholar, Immanuel Kant. Bailey does, however, take these fundamental liberal ideas further by adding three characteristics to the description of a liberal education. These are: *fundamentality and generality*; *instrinsically valued ends*; and *reason*.

### Fundamentality and generality

These terms describe the type of knowledge developed in a liberal education. Fundamental knowledge is foundational. It is the type of knowledge, as the name implies, that can be built upon. It is necessary for increasingly complex learning and allows for conceptual progression. It focuses more on content knowledge (knowing *that*) than activity (or knowing *how*). Bailey provides an example of foundational knowledge by differentiating it from the specific and limiting "how to" knowledge. For example, toffee can be made by following a specific recipe that tells the maker what ingredients are to be used, how they are to be put together, and what temperatures are to be used in order to get a specific outcome. Following the recipe precisely should yield the same results every time. The maker will know how to make toffee. It requires the maker to *follow* rather than think or create. Compare this *how-to* knowledge with knowledge about the properties of sugar. "Knowing that" sugar is soft and flexible at 115 degrees Celsius, cracks at 150 degrees, and caramelises at 180 provides the kind of knowledge which requires the maker to think and provides possibilities to create. This type of knowledge can be built upon by generalising the knowledge to other contexts. Bailey argues that knowledge must be as fundamental as possible to allow for generality. Such knowledge is *more* rather than *less* liberal. Furthermore, general principles are more fundamental than the particulars that are subsumed under them.

Fundamentality as a characteristic of a liberal education is not, therefore, related to what has come to be known in education as "the basics". That is not to say that learning to read and use a recipe or to learn by rote the basics of numeracy and literacy are not useful. They are steps for the learner to move to more abstracted and generalisable ideas that can be applied in other contexts. The generalisability of knowledge has been described as "conceptual progression" (McPhail & Rata, 2016; Rata, 2016; Winch, 2013), which is the idea that as students advance, a foundation in lower-order concepts is required for conceptual progression (i.e., learning), to occur.

### *Intrinsically valued ends*

The third characteristic of a liberal education is its intrinsic motivation and value. Understanding that which is intrinsically valuable also requires an understanding of that which is "instrumental". Something can be said to be instrumental when it is the means to which an end or outcome is achieved. The instrumental, then, is only valued because the end is valued; for example, schooling is often seen as valuable because it can lead to a good career or getting into university. The good career or entrance into a desirable university programme are the valued ends. Attending school is only valued because it is instrumental to that end; it is not valued for itself but what it can lead to. In 2015, New Zealand's then Minister of Tertiary Education, Stephen Joyce, announced that from 2017 all universities, wānanga, polytechnics and funded private training establishments would be required to publish information about the employment status and earnings of their graduates broken down by specific degrees and diplomas (New Zealand Government, 2015). This information, Joyce explained, would assist high school students to make better choices about and benefit more from the courses they study. The primary motivation for course selection in higher education are, from Joyce's view, external—the expectation of a good income level. Intrinsic motivation for course selection would include reasons inherent to the task itself such as interest, intellectual curiosity, or even enjoyment.

A liberal education is concerned for the intrinsically worthwhile. The criticism is that this is a luxury that only the wealthy can afford and hence the accusations that liberal education is elitist. While there is truth to this criticism, a return to the concept of equality as a defining characteristic of liberalism is also central to a democratic society. Bailey warns "if a society becomes solely concerned with wealth production and no longer sees education as concerned with ends, then all becomes caught up in a pointless and particularly alienating circle" (1984, p. 24).

### Reason

The final characteristic of a liberal education is the development of reason. The development of reason is linked to the principles of liberation or freedom. Bailey (1984) argues that "only reason can liberate one from the present and the particular" (p. 24). Being able to act and understand beyond the initial impulses of emotion contributes to the self-governing individual that Thomas Jefferson referred to some 200 years ago. Underlying this focus on the self is the belief that "society has the most to gain by maximizing the self-knowledge and resources of the individuals that make it up" (Hill, 1994, p. 100). It emphasises the role of individuals in a democratic society—those who can decide and make choices based on what comes from themselves not from the dictates of others.

Liberal education, then, is concerned with liberation and equality through the development of reason, a focus on that which has intrinsic value, and that which can be generalised beyond the setting in which it was learned.

## Conclusion

When positioned alongside the philosophies, educational traditions, and contemporary issues presented in this book, liberal education is often viewed as an elite and traditional approach to schooling which has been eclipsed by more "relevant" and empowering approaches. This chapter proposes a return to an understanding of liberal education as *liberating* by revisiting its philosophical and political roots. The concepts of liberty and equality that underpin liberal philosophical and political theory are contested and represented differently in educational policy, curriculum, and practice. I have presented a view of liberty where fundamental knowledge based in academic subjects acts as a liberating factor in schooling. Learners are liberated from the limitations of relevance. They are able to learn that which is beyond their experience. Furthermore, I have argued that all students should have access to this type of knowledge if education is to fulfil egalitarian principles. A commitment to individuals and the acknowledgement of their differences allows for the expectation of different outcomes but does not undermine the idea that all children have the right to educational opportunities that will allow them to reach their full potential. This is the goal of education and it is both uplifting and daunting. It requires moving beyond that which we not only, to return to Kant's words, dare to know, but dare to hope!

## *References*

Bailey, C. (1984). *Beyond the present and the particular: A theory of liberal education.* London, UK: Routledge & Kegan Paul.

Barrett, B. D. (2017). Bernstein in the urban classroom: A case study. *British Journal of Sociology of Education*, 1–14.

Barrett, B. D., & Rata, E. (2014). *Knowledge and the future of the curriculum.* New York, NY: Palgrave Macmillan.

Beck, J. (2013). Powerful knowledge, esoteric knowledge, curriculum knowledge. *Cambridge Journal of Education*, *43*(2), 177–193.

Codd, J. (2005). Teachers as "managed professionals" in the global education industry: The New Zealand experience. *Educational Review*, *57*(2), 193–206.

Codd, J. (2008). Neoliberalism, globalisation and the deprofessionalisation of teachers. In V. Carpenter, M. Stephenson, P. Roberts, & J. Jesson (Eds.), *Ngā kaupapa here: Connections and contradictions in education* (pp. 14–24). Melbourne, VIC: Cengage Learning.

Crittenden, B. (2006). The school curriculum and liberal education. *Education Research and Perspectives*, *33*(1), 105–127.

Falk, J., Hampton, G., Hodgkinson, A., Parker, K., & Rorris, A. (1993). *Social equity and the urban environment.* Report to the Commonwealth Environment Protection Agency. Canberra, ACT: AGPS.

Fraser, P. (1939) Department of Education annual report, Appendices to the Journal of the House of Representatives [AJHR], E1.

Fromm, E. (1956). *The sane society.* London, UK: Routledge & Kegan Paul.

Hill, B. V. (1994). *Teaching secondary social studies in a multicultural society.* Melbourne, VIC: Longman Cheshire.

Hirst, P. H. (2010). Liberal education and the nature of knowledge. In R.F. Dearen, P.H. Hirst & R.S. Peters (Eds.) *Education and the development of reason*. London: Routledge & Kegan Paul. (Original work published 1972).

Kant, E. (1784/1995). What is Enlightenment? In I. Kramnick (Ed.), *The portable enlightenment reader* (pp. 1–6). New York, NY: Penguin. (Original work published 1784).

Jonathon, R. (1997). Liberalism and education. *Journal of Philosophy of Education, 31*(1), 181–216.

Lalor, J. J. (Ed.). (1899). *Cyclopædia of political science, political economy, and of the political history of the United States, by the best American and European writers* (Vol. 2). Chicago, IL: Maynard, Merrill, & Company.

Locke, J. (1988). *Two Treatises of Government*. Cambridge, UK: Cambridge University Press. (Original work published 1772).

McPhail, G., & Rata, E. (2016). Comparing curriculum types: 'Powerful knowledge' and '21st century learning'. *New Zealand Journal of Educational Studies, 51*(1), 53–68.

Mill, J. S. (2002). *On liberty*. New York, NY: Dover Books. (Original work published 1859).

Moore, R. (2013). Social realism and the problem of the problem of knowledge in the sociology of education. *British Journal of Sociology of Education, 34*(3), 333–353.

New Zealand Government. (14 September, 2015). Employment outcomes to be published. Retrieved from http://www.beehive.govt.nz/release/employment-outcomes-be-published

Nussbaum, M. (2004). Liberal education and global community. *Liberal Education, 90*(1), 42–47.

Pitkin, H. F. (1988). Are freedom and liberty twins? *Political Theory, 16*(4), 523–552.

Rata, E. (2012). The politics of knowledge in education. *British Educational Research Journal, 38*(1), 103–124.

Rata, E. (2016). A pedagogy of conceptual progression and the case for academic knowledge. *British Educational Research Journal, 42*(1), 168–184.

Ravitch, D. (2001). Education and democracy. In D. Ravitch & J. Viteretti (Eds.), *Making good citizens: Education and civil society* (pp. 15–29). New Haven, CT: Yale University Press.

Tuckness, A. (2016). Locke's political philosophy. In E. N. Zalta (Ed.), *The Stanford encyclopedia of philosophy*. Retrieved from https://plato.stanford.edu/archives/spr2016/entries/locke-political/

Winch, C. (2013). Curriculum design and epistemic ascent. *Journal of Philosophy of Education, 47*(1), 128–146.

Wollstonecraft, M. (2001). *A vindication of the rights of men and a vindication of the rights of woman.* Blacksburg, VA: Virginia Tech. (Original work published 1798).

Young, M. (2008). From constructivism to realism in the sociology of the curriculum. *Review of Research in Education, 32*(1), 1–28.

Young, M. (2010). Why educators must differentiate knowledge from experience. *Pacific-Asian Education, 22*(1), 9–20.

Young, M., & Muller, J. (2013). On the powers of powerful knowledge. *Review of Education, 1*(3), 229–250.

THINKING ABOUT LIBERALISM AND
PROGRESSIVISM IN TODAY'S WORLD

## Chapter 5  Rethinking what it means to be a teacher through a mixed modality approach

Graham McPhail

*School of Curriculum and Pedagogy*
*Faculty of Education and Social Work*
*The University of Auckland*

**Abstract**

This chapter draws on the ideas developed in the prior chapters but rather than recreating a dichotomy of "progressive versus liberal" or "curriculum versus pedagogy" it offers a fresh way of looking at what the traditions can offer each other for the betterment of teaching and learning. Using five pedagogical constructs from Basil Bernstein—selection, sequence, pacing, evaluation, and interaction—it promotes a mixed modality approach in which curriculum is knowledge-centred and pedagogy is student-centred and teachers are leaders of learning.

**Key words**
Liberal—progressive—disciplinary knowledge—curriculum—pedagogy—mixed modality

## *Introduction*

For a century or more, debates about the central purpose of education have tended to oscillate between two long-standing, apparently contradictory, traditions. In one view, it is argued that education's purpose is to build students' intellectual capacity through exposure to certain kinds of knowledge: "the best that has been thought and said" (Arnold, 1869/1960, p. 6). In this argument, often termed "liberal education" (or knowledge, or subject-centred), rather than the learner, takes centre-stage. This knowledge approach has tended to be associated with a negative view of the curriculum as unchanging; a "one-size fits all" bank of facts taught through a rote-learning pedagogy. At a deeper level, this view of education is seen by many as engendering a problematic unquestioning and uncritical respect for authority and traditional values.

In the second view, termed "progressive" (or student-centred), the child's personal social and learning needs come first. Supporters of this view often suggest that education is not about learning "things" but about "learning how to learn". The curriculum is much more open to everyday knowledge, content is not specified, and there is an emphasis on developing generic and "therapeutic" aspects of education, such as "key competencies". The child's experience and interests are used to generate curriculum content and, in terms of pedagogy, the teacher becomes a facilitator and "co-constructs" knowledge with the student (see, for example, O'Connor & Greenslade, 2012).

In this chapter I am going to suggest that neither tradition is sufficient in providing us with the rationale to develop a truly "progressive" philosophy for teaching practice in the 21st century. The traditions, and the politics that accumulates around them, encourage us to think in polarised ways but I am going to suggest that each tradition contains elements of "truth", but that no one tradition has all the answers. By drawing on dimensions from liberal, progressive, critical, and more recent social realist views of education, I will argue that to be progressive, to be student-centred, and critical, firstly requires us to be "knowledge-focused"; to be clear about what it is we want our students to learn. The first idea I will introduce to support my argument is that of making a clear distinction between *curriculum* and *pedagogy*. This will provide us with a means to think clearly about the differences between *what* we choose to teach and *how* we go about teaching it. Secondly, I will introduce the idea there are two types of knowledge in the world—everyday and disciplinary—and to be able to distinguish between them is vitally important for education; it can lead us to identify some knowledge as particularly powerful for educational contexts. Finally, I will outline what is termed a "mixed modality" approach for teaching. This approach draws on both traditional and progressive educational ideas. My aim is to convince you that it is a mixed modality approach that will enable us to rethink what it means to be a progressive teacher for the 21st century.

## The pedagogy/curriculum distinction

While in practice *what* we teach (what I will call "the curriculum") and *how* we teach (what I will call "pedagogy") should be intimately related and in balance with each other, over recent decades *how we teach* has gained prominence over considering *what we teach* and the relationship between the two (Hayes, 2017). If you are a recent teacher graduate, or are currently undertaking teacher training, think for a moment about the amount of time given in your course to these two aspects. Biesta (2012) has coined the term "learnification" to describe this trend of focusing almost exclusively on how to teach at the expense of what it is we are teaching. He argues that these ideas about the importance of pedagogy (the how) have become so pervasive that the what of learning has become next to invisible and the teacher has started to vanish with it (Biesta, 2012). Instead, he argues, "the point of education is never that children or students learn, but they learn *something*, that they learn this for particular *purposes*, and that they learn this from *someone*" (2012, p. 36, emphases in original).

Pedagogic expertise is vitally important. It provides the means for considering how best to sequence and pace teaching for particular contexts, and also the means for developing ways to motivate and engage students. However, pedagogy is only half the story. Pedagogy must be a carrier of something; the knowledge chosen by the teacher as most important to learn. *What* we teach should in turn influence *how* we teach it. For example, if the content of a particular subject or knowledge area is structured in a way where the sequence of concepts is vital for understanding—in maths or in English grammar, for example—then this will influence the pedagogy. In these examples, because the structure of the knowledge itself is sequential, the pedagogy may need to be more teacher-led. On the other hand, in a social studies or arts context, for example, students may be given more 'freedom' to research and explore aspects of the curriculum for themselves and to also draw on their personal and everyday knowledge. Here we can begin to see the relationship between what is being taught and how it is taught. In either case, the teacher needs to know what it is that they want their students to learn. An effective teacher needs to continually ask, "What are the concepts, ideas, or skills I am wanting my students to learn?" Only then can they ask pedagogical questions such as "How might I best go about teaching this content?" Young and Lambert (2014) argue that thinking in this way about curriculum and pedagogy as having different purposes is vital:

> … the curriculum needs to be seen as having a purpose of its own: the intellectual development of students. It should not be treated as a means for motivating students or for solving social problems … The curriculum should exclude the everyday knowledge of students, whereas that knowledge is a resource for the pedagogic work of teachers. Students do not come to school to learn what they already know. (pp. 96–97)

## *Types of knowledge*

The quote from Young and Lambert highlights the second major idea of this chapter; that there are two types of human knowledge and that we need to be aware of the difference to enable effective student learning (Young, 2010a, 2010b, 2013). It is not that one type is *better* than another, but each provides *different* affordances for learning. The two types are known by various names but here I will use "everyday knowledge" and "disciplinary knowledge". Everyday knowledge is acquired in an ad hoc way and lacks any underlying structure (e.g., learning to tie your shoelaces, or gradually becoming aware of roles and relationships in a family), whereas disciplinary knowledge is structured *with concepts that have interrelationships.* While we meet disciplinary knowledge organised in school subjects, the source of the knowledge is in the disciplines developed over time in various inter-generational and international research communities (e.g., physics, music, biology, economics, etc.). As I explain more fully later, disciplinary knowledge should comprise the *curriculum content* and everyday knowledge can be used as a *pedagogic resource* to help motivate students and to make connections between what they already know and what they are learning at school (Rata, 2012; Vygotsky, 1986; Young, 2010a, 2010b, 2013; Young & Lambert, 2014).

Vygotsky and Dewey, both regarded as progressive educators, were nevertheless very aware of the distinction between everyday and disciplinary knowledge. For example, Vygotsky (1986) called the knowledge types "scientific" and "spontaneous". He argues that it is the role of the teacher to introduce students to the more systemised scientific concepts. In contrast, spontaneous concepts "are the result of experience in the absence of systematic instruction … such concepts are unsystematic, not conscious, and often wrong" (Karpov, 2003, p. 65). Despite the emphasis Dewey (1938) placed on incorporating student experience into educational contexts, he was also clear that utilising experience was a complex rather than a straightforward challenge for teachers and that the curriculum should be designed to lead students towards disciplinary knowledge. Two quotes from his 1938 book *Experience and Education* make these matters clear:

> The belief that all genuine education comes about through experience does not mean all experiences are genuinely or equally educative … for some experiences are mis-educative. Any experience is mis-educative that has the effect of arresting or distorting the growth of further experience. (p. 25)

> But finding the material for learning within experience is only the first step. The next step is the progressive development of what is already experienced into a fuller and richer and also more organised form, a form that gradually approximates that in which subject-matter is presented to the skilled, mature person. (p. 73)

While always developing—dynamic rather than static—the disciplines provide us with a reservoir of ideas and concepts for developing human thinking in systematic ways which everyday knowledge does not. This is why it is so important to introduce students to disciplinary concepts; it develops their ability to think systematically and abstractly. Drawing directly on Vygotsky, Karpov (2003) and Rata (2016) point out that the acquisition of scientific concepts transforms students' thinking and their understanding of their spontaneous or everyday thoughts and experiences: "students' spontaneous concepts become structured and conscious … as a result, students' thinking becomes much more independent of their personal experience. They … develop the ability to operate at the level of formal-logical thought" (Karpov, 2003, p. 66).

## *Powerful knowledge*

More recently, Young and Muller (2013) and other educational researchers have explored the idea that some knowledges are more powerful than others in the ways in which they can give *power to* students to enable their development as thinkers and critical interpreters of the world around them. Young and Muller argue that powerful knowledge is powerful because it enables the development of new ways of thinking as we come into contact with the structure, specialisation, and emergent qualities of this type of knowledge. By "emergent", Young and Muller (2013) mean the potential of concepts to create new knowledge; a creative potential as knowledge is put to use by students. For example, in a music classroom we could learn to perform songs and play the ukulele (rather like rote learning) but, if at some point, students are introduced to the systems of meaning of the subject, such as musical structures and harmony, they may become knowledge *producers* themselves; in this case, composers. Maude (2016) suggests powerful knowledge enables students to:

> … discover new ways of thinking, better explain and understand the natural and social worlds, think about alternative futures and what they could do to influence them, have some power over their own knowledge, be able to engage in current debates of significance, and go beyond the limits of their personal experience. (p. 72)

Disciplinary knowledge is also more useful than an everyday knowledge or opinion as it provides the means to generalise and abstract from the particular.

The concept of powerful knowledge has emerged in response to the world-wide trend towards learnification discussed above, and the idea that everyday knowledge and disciplinary knowledge offer equal affordances for learning. In New Zealand, this idea has been termed "knowledge equivalence" (Taylor, 2014) or "parity of esteem" (Hipkins, Johnston, & Sheehan, 2016) and it was motivated by the need to broaden the ways in which success could be recognised in the education system. However, in many instances, knowledge equivalence has resulted in a misleading idea that different types of knowledge offer equivalent learning affordances and career pathways (Rata & Taylor, 2015). The social realist argument (Barrett & Rata, 2014; Maton & Moore, 2010; Young, 2008) is that some knowledge is more powerful for learning than other forms and that all students have a right of access to this more powerful knowledge (Young, 2013).

If we accept this argument in favour of the importance of abstract, conceptual, disciplinary knowledge, then the increasing emphasis in teacher preparation (and in the educational literature on pedagogy) and the importance of students' personal, cultural, social, everyday knowledge seems somewhat misguided. The important point to note is that student's everyday knowledge is important as a *pedagogic resource* as the teacher gets to know the student as a learner. The teacher can then use everyday knowledge as a means to connect what students already know with what they are learning. The students' everyday knowledge will seldom be a reliable resource for *curriculum content*.

## A mixed modality approach

A great deal of longitudinal research in primary school science carried out by Morais and Neves (2001, 2011) has developed a model of practice that has been effective for all students without lessening the level of demand in the curriculum content. These researchers state that "we have come to a model that conceptualises a school pedagogic practice that [has] the potential to lead children to success at school, narrowing the gap between children from differentiated backgrounds" (2011, p. 191). Their model uses Bernstein's (1975/2003) five fundamental dimensions of pedagogic practice: *selection*, *sequence*, *pacing*, *evaluation*, and *teacher/student model*, and utilises approaches more often associated with progressive pedagogy in relation to pacing and the teacher/student model and more traditional pedagogy for selection, sequence, and evaluation (see Figure 5.1). Each dimension is now considered in turn.

Figure 5.1 *A mixed modality approach to teaching*

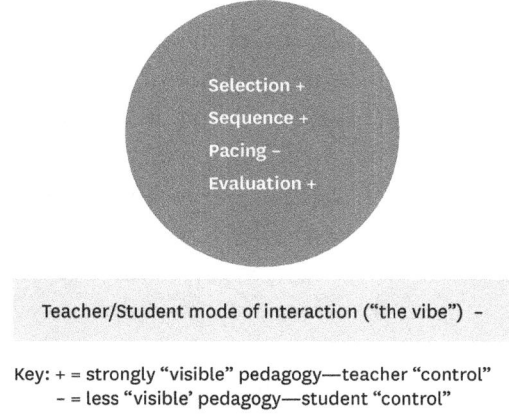

Key: + = strongly "visible" pedagogy—teacher "control"
– = less "visible' pedagogy—student "control"

Source: Morais and Neves (2001, 2011)

## Selection

The teacher, as more knowledgeable than the students, determines *what* is to be learnt. This involves having big-picture knowledge of the subject, and being able to choose the most appropriate content for teaching the chosen concepts. To do this, the teacher must know the content of the subjects well, know what is appropriate for the curriculum level, and know what conceptual problems are likely to be encountered; for example, common misconception or concepts students find difficult. Once the concepts and content are chosen, the teacher can then begin to consider what engaging pedagogies might be used to stimulate student interest; for example, posing a guiding question, relating the concepts to be learnt to a theme, or a real-world concept.

## Sequence

Again, the teacher, as more knowledgeable than the student, needs to determine the broad, and sometimes detailed, sequence of what is being covered in a particular learning context. In some subjects, sequence is more significant than others; for example, in maths we must learn addition before division. In most subjects, there will be a relationship between the key concepts that suggests a logical order in which the concepts relate to each other to make a whole. For example, it would be logical to study the concept of ecosystems before studying sustainability, and within each main or higher-order concept there will be a sequence of lower-order concepts. For instance, an ecosystem study would be likely to involve coverage of a sequence of key concepts such as biotic and abiotic categorisations, food chains, food webs, energy transformations, and biogeochemical cycling. According to Vygotsky (1986/1934), the process of teaching and sequencing concepts involves first introducing a sense of the whole along with the key concept, breaking it down into its parts, reassembling, and then relating the concept(s) to possible student experiences and knowledge. This new knowledge transforms the students' everyday knowledge. This approach utilises the two very important ideas introduced above: different types of knowledge (spontaneous and everyday) and the influence of structure of the knowledge on pedagogy (Karpov, 2003; Rata, 2016).

*Pacing*
Ideally, this is one dimension where students should be given more *control*. Students require time to assimilate and develop understanding of the knowledge in hand and the chance to revisit key ideas and applications of knowledge. Students need to be given some control over this time. But, "time without explicit criteria may be useless" (Morais, 2002, p. 560).

*Evaluation*
This involves the teacher making explicit to students what is required to achieve a certain task or understanding. It is Hattie and Timperley's (2007) model of feedback: "Where am I going?", "How am I going?", and "What do I need to do next?" This is the most crucial aspect of teaching and it requires that the teacher actually knows the next step in the search for quality or understanding, and an appropriate pedagogical approach for bringing this about.

*Teacher/student mode of interaction*
Underpinning the earlier-listed dimensions is a certain sort of teacher/student mode of interaction developed by each teacher according to

their personality and approach (the classroom vibe). This could range from more formal to informal, but Morais and Neves's (2011) research suggests it should involve developing a personalised attitude to students and a learning environment where students can feel confident to "question, discuss, and share ideas, thus strengthening the impact of the evaluative criteria" (Morais, 2002, p. 561).

It should be clear from these explanations that a mixed modality practice utilises certain approaches more often aligned with progressivism and some more aligned with traditionalism. Such an approach is centred on students' development in relation to their interaction with knowledge rather than in pre-aligning practice with a particular tradition; it allows us to move the theorising of practice away from progressive/traditional dichotomies (McPhail, 2013).

## *Conclusion*

The limitations of traditional and progressive views were clear to Dewey (1938) when he noted that humans tend to think in terms of opposites. The editor of Dewey's publication *Experience and Education* summarises the positions well. Although written in 1938, it seems as if his comments could be directed at us in the present day:

> Where the traditional school relied on subjects or the cultural heritage for its content, the "new" school has exalted the learner's impulse and interest … neither of these sets of values is sufficient unto itself. Both are essential … the traditional curriculum undoubtedly entailed rigid regimentation and a discipline that ignored the capacities and interests of child nature. Today, however, the reaction to this type of schooling often fosters the other extreme—incoherent curriculum, excessive individualism, and a spontaneity which is a deception of freedom. Dr Dewey insists that neither the old nor the new education is adequate. (Hall-Quest, 1938, pp. 9–10)

In this chapter I have attempted to reclaim the label "progressive" for an approach to teaching that is not limited by either/or positions that we often hear expressed in "bi-polar slogans" that offer us a stark choice between "child-centred" or "subject-centred"; "traditional or progressive"; "teaching facts" or "learning how to learn". This is the result of an over-simplistic view that one approach is right for all occasions in all contexts. My assertion is that we need to be as progressive as we can as pedagogues; to be imaginative and creative in the ways we engage students with the challenges of learning about *things*. In relation to curriculum content, we need to be more traditional in the sense that students need to come into contact with established bodies of knowledge that are quite different from their everyday knowledge. In other words, the curriculum should be knowledge-centred and pedagogy should be student-centred.

The argument for forms of engaging pedagogy and the way in which knowledge is seen as emergent rather than always clearly defined, separates this social realist view from that of the liberal tradition (see Siteine, Chapter 4 of this book), although they have much in common. This social realist view is progressive in that it aims to see students actively engaged in learning while providing them with access to the realms of disciplinary thought out there in the wide world. In other words, to be knowledge-centred is to be student-centred. This requires teachers to be to be leaders of learning, rather than facilitators. To think children can "discover" knowledge for themselves with a facilitator teacher is a romantic notion that runs the risk of teachers abdicating their responsibilities. Teachers need to know the conceptual destination of the learning journeys and guide students through engaging pedagogies towards the powerful knowledge that enables them to learn to think and reason, and to imagine worlds beyond their experience.

**Note**
1. The term "scientific" here is used by Vygotsky in a broad sense as referring to systemised forms of disciplinary knowledge, found not only in the sciences but also in the social sciences, humanities and the arts.

## *References*
Arnold, M. (1960). *Culture and anarchy*. London, UK: Cambridge University Press. (Original work published 1869).

Barrett, B., & Rata, E. (Eds.). (2016). *Knowledge and the future of the curriculum: International studies in social realism*. Houndmills, UK: Palgrave Macmillan.

Bernstein, B. (2003). *Class, codes and control (Vol. 3): Towards a theory of educational transmission.* London, UK: Routledge. (Original work published 1975).

Biesta, G. (2012). Giving teaching back to education: Responding to the disappearance of the teacher. *Phenomenology and Practice, 6*(2), 35–49.

Dewey, J. (1938/1997) *Experience and education.* New York, NY: Touchstone.

Hall-Quest, A. (1938). Editorial foreword. In J. Dewey, *Experience and Education.* New York, NY: Touchstone.

Hattie, J., & Timperley, H. (2007). The power of feedback. *Review of Educational Research, 77*(1), 81–112.

Hayes, D. (2017). *Seven ways education needs to change in 2017. The conversation.* Retrieved from http://theconversation.com/seven-ways-education-needs-to-change-in-2017-70821

Hipkins, R., Johnston, M., & Sheehan, M. (2016). *NCEA in context.* Wellington: NZCER Press.

Karpov, Y. (2003). Vygotsky's doctrine of scientific concepts: Its role for contemporary education. In A. Kozulin, B. Gindis, V. Ageyev, & S. Miller (Eds.), *Vygotsky's educational theory in cultural context* (pp. 65–82). Cambridge, UK: Cambridge University Press.

Maton, K., & Moore, R. (Eds.). (2010). *Social realism, knowledge and the sociology of education: Coalitions of the mind.* London, UK: Continuum.

Maude, A. (2016). What might powerful geographical knowledge look like? *Geography, 101*(2), 70–76.

McPhail, G. (2013). Mixed pedagogic modalities: The potential for increased student engagement and success. *New Zealand Journal of Educational Studies, 48*(1), 113–126.

Morais, A. M. (2002). Basil Bernstein at the micro level of the classroom. *British Journal of Sociology of Education, 23*(4), 559–569.

Morais, A. M., & Neves, I. P. (2001). Pedagogic social contexts: Studies for a sociology of learning. In A. Morais, I. Neves, B. Davies, & H. Daniels (Eds.), *Towards a sociology of pedagogy: The contribution of Basil Bernstein to research* (pp. 185–221). New York, NY: Lang.

Morais, A. M., & Neves, I. P. (2011). Educational texts and contexts that work: Discussing the optimization of a model of pedagogic practice. In D. Frandji & P. Vitale (Eds.), *Knowledge, pedagogy and society: International perspectives on Basil Bernstein's sociology of education* (pp. 191–211). London,

UK: Routledge. Retrieved from http://essa.ie.ulisboa.pt/ficheiros/artigos/livros/2011_Educationaltextsandcontextsthatwork.pdf

O'Connor, N., & Greenslade, S. (2012). Co-constructed pathways of learning: A case study. *set: Research Information for Teachers*, *1*, 49–55.

Rata, E. (2012). *The politics of knowledge in education*. London, UK: Routledge.

Rata, E. (2016). A pedagogy of conceptual progression and the case for academic knowledge. *British Journal of Educational Research*, *42*(1), 168–184.

Rata, E., & Taylor, A. (2015). Knowledge equivalence discourse in New Zealand secondary school science. *New Zealand Journal of Educational Studies*, *50*(2), 223–238.

Taylor, A. (2014). *Students' search for identity as credit hunters or science students*. Unpublished master's thesis, The University of Auckland. Retrieved from https://researchspace.auckland.ac.nz/handle/2292/26365

Vygotsky, L. (1986). *Thought and language*. Cambridge, MA: The MIT Press. (Original work published 1934).

Young, M. (2010a). Why educators must differentiate knowledge from experience. *Pacific Asian Education*, *22*, 9–20. Retrieved from http://pacificcircleconsortium.org/PAEJournal.html

Young, M. (2010b). The future of education in a knowledge society: The radical case for a subject-based curriculum. *Pacific Asian Education*, *22*, 21–32. Retrieved from http://pacificcircleconsortium.org/PAEJournal.html

Young, M. (2013). Overcoming the crisis in curriculum theory: A knowledge-based approach. *Journal of Curriculum Studies*, *45*(2), 101–118.

Young, M. F. D. (2008). *Bringing knowledge back in: From social constructivism to social realism in the sociology of education*. London, UK: Routledge.

Young, M., & Lambert, D. (2014). *Knowledge and the future school: Curriculum and social justice*. London, UK: Bloomsbury.

Young, M., & Muller, J. (2013). On the powers of powerful knowledge. *Review of Education*, *1*(3), 229–250.

## Liberalism Discussion starters

1. What are the most enduring aspects of a liberal education prevalent in today's education system? Why have these ideas endured? What developments or adaptations have occurred in liberal education thinking?
2. Explain what is meant by Bailey's idea of education as a means of liberating individuals from "the present and particular" of their birth? How might education do this? How well is it succeeding in achieving this?
3. What would you consider should be included in powerful knowledge? Why is it powerful?
4. In what ways does the idea of combining a knowledge-centered curriculum and student-centered pedagogy reflect liberal ideas about education?

TRADITION 3: SOCIALLY CRITICAL
PERSPECTIVES

# Socially critical perspectives—a personal reflection

## Fetaui Iosefo

*School of Critical Studies in Education*
*Faculty of Education and Social Work*
*The University of Auckland*

## *Introduction*

This reflective (and reflexive) piece begins from the perspective of a Bachelor of Education student. It explores her first encounter as an undergraduate student with critical theory and kaupapa Māori theory. It explores the relationship between both theories and exposes the influence on her identity as a hybrid. It discusses the influence these theories had on her as a graduated teacher. This reflection positions both of these theories as sites of struggle, resistance, and emancipation. The search for voice and choice is threaded throughout this piece by means of time (18 years).

## *Voice and choice*

As a Samoan woman born in Aotearoa New Zealand, raised in South Auckland, negotiating how much voice and how much choice you have is filled with complexities. Growing up in a religious, Samoan home meant that children were seen and not heard. With this same ideology, we were sent to school with firm instructions to be quiet, obedient, and never to ask any questions. If you asked any questions, this was deemed to be a sign of disrespect. Being raised in the wake of the "Dawn Raids" in New Zealand consolidated the importance of staying silent. It confirmed that our "voices" did not matter in this society which ultimately silenced my voice and opened a plethora of uncertainties and insecurities. My educational experience reflected this and I became a stereotypical "brown brother" high school dropout statistic, pregnant at 19. At the age of 27, I re-entered education under the "special admissions" label and began my Bachelor of Education through The University of Auckland on our Manukau campus.

My first encounter with critical theory (Apple, 1979; Freire, 1996; Kincheloe & McLaren, 2002) alongside kaupapa Māori theory (Pihama, 1993; Smith, 1999) was in my first year of the Bachelor of Education. These foreign terms were introduced to us by Maxine Stephenson, Kuni Jenkins, Margie Hohepa, Glenys Paraha, and Leonie Pihama. These women, to say the least, were a powerful combination of awesomeness. They introduced notions of power, control, and social justice which challenged my understanding of silent voices and choices. I began to question: "Where did power come from?", "Who was controlling who?", "What was social justice?", and "Did I have power?" These questions troubled my world view of being quiet, obedient, and not questioning.

Critical theory began to unpack my choice of remaining silent, remaining voiceless. Giroux (1984) discusses critical theory as being a site of struggle for a better world. Understanding this charged me with new excitement as I began to understand that to question wasn't a bad thing. The possibilities of questioning could lead to understanding, and understanding could lead to the betterment of our world. Although as insightful as this was, I could not see how I could implement this perspective in my own life where questioning was non-negotiable. How do you go from not questioning to questioning? As this reflective process began to take place, it took into account that my silence was a reflection of my positionality as a Samoan woman born in Aotearoa; living on the "South-side". Realisation began to dawn that my silence was a reflection of colonisation, marginalisation, and oppression. Fay (1993) confirmed what these papers, grounded in critical theory, were doing to me. They were "raising the consciousness of the oppressed". Not only was I "woken" to being physically different, my mindset was different. This complements Young's (1990) proposition for us to view and understand difference, domination, and oppression. Once we can see this, then we are to seek justice. In seeking justice, we seek emancipation.

My encounter with the kaupapa Māori theory was critical theory in praxis. Pihama (1993) suggests that kaupapa Māori theory analyses dominance, power, and societal inequalities and, therefore, aligns with critical theory. Kaupapa Māori theory brought to life the experience of Māori in Aotearoa, up close and personal. Each of the lecturers discussed the silencing of Māori, inculcation of Māori, and the causes of trauma for Māori. Furthermore, they equally brought to light the self-determination of Māori to (re)claim, transform, and emancipate. Kaupapa Māori validated Māori epistemologies and ontologies because it was *by* Māori *for* Māori.

This learning had a profound effect on the shaping of my own identity. I sat in every class in awe, that, right in front of me, I was seeing critical theory in action. I was witnessing the emancipation process and experiencing critical pedagogy right before my very eyes. In Iosefo (2016), I discuss the experience of having to sit a Māori IQ test and how everyone in that class failed. The exercise was, for me and my fellow classmates, to feel for a moment what it would have been like as a Māori student being educated in a Pākehā society. This experience was a powerful teaching moment. I felt a gut-wrenching sadness for Māori and a strong surge of social justice for Māori children, for all the children that I would one day teach. I became determined to always place myself in the shoes of each child in every class I taught. This became part of my sacred duty.

Once graduated, my teaching philosophy, influenced by critical theory and kaupapa Māori theory, began to evolve. I embraced the pedagogy of the oppressed (Freire, 1996) and pedagogy of hope (hooks, 2003). One particular notion that resonated with me was hooks' (1994) "holistic" education. Holistic education encourages each student to identify themselves within education. When students can see themselves as an important part of education they are then able to make meaning by making connections between themselves, family, community, and globally. Critical theory and kaupapa Māori theory underpin both holistic education and critical literacy. Collectively, they became an integral part of pedagogy.

Within my practice, critical literacy was a vehicle for my students to explore the voices that had been silenced. They imagined what the silent voices would say if they had a choice to be part of the discussion. Freire (1996) argues that relationships of the powerful and dominant over the marginalised and oppressed are because of the lack of voice and, most importantly, the lack of dialogue. In this process, we must be aware of power relations. As a teacher, creating an environment where questioning and robust dialogue were the norm was tremendously exciting. Hearing the voices of children and working *with* them to extend their knowledge in all the curriculum areas and expanding their skills of inquiry was, and is, part of critical theory's empowerment and emancipatory process.

Time has passed and 18 years have elapsed since my first encounter with critical theory and kaupapa Māori theory. Three things are for sure. First, I have aged. Secondly, the same passion and conviction I encountered 18 years ago is very much, if not more, still burning in my belly. Thirdly, I have witnessed kaupapa Māori theory become a beacon of transformative hope, nationally and globally for all indigenous voices—for all marginalised and oppressed voices.

Finally, because of my experience with critical theory and kaupapa Māori theory, I have chosen to find my voice, that is, who *I am* as a Samoan woman born in Aotearoa. The Samoan philosopher and scholar, Tui Atua Tamasese Efi (2014), encourages us all to have a voice, even if it means that you whisper. So as a mother, wife, daughter, sister, and teacher I acknowledge the following:

***Voice and choice***
It is in your voice
It is in your choice
Choose to be silent
Choose to whisper
Choice is your voice
Voice your choice
Today my voice of choice
… is to "whisper".

JoFI

## *References*

Apple, M. (1979). On analysing hegemony. In M. Apple (Ed.), *Ideology and curriculum* (pp. 1–25). London, UK: Routledge & Kegan Paul.

Efi, His Excellency Tui Atua Tapua Tamasese Ta'isi (2014). Whispers and vanities in Samoan indigenous religious culture. In Suaalii-Sauni T. M., Wendt M. A., Mo'a V., Fuamatu N., Va'ai U. L., Whaitiri R., & Filipo S. L. (Eds.), *Whispers and vanities: Samoan indigenous knowledge and religion.* Wellington: Huia Publishers.

Fay, B. (1993). The elements of critical social science. In M. Hammersley (Ed.), *Social research: Philosophy politics and practice* (pp. 33–36). London, UK: Sage.

Freire, P. (1996). *Pedagogy of the oppressed.* London, UK: Penguin Books.

Giroux, H. (1984). *Critical theory and educational practice.* Melbourne, VIC: Deakin University Press.

hooks, bell. (1994). *Teaching to transgress: Education as a practice of free.* New York, NY: Routledge.

hooks, bell. (2003). *Teaching community: A pedagogy of hope.* Manhattan, NY: Routledge.

Iosefo, F. (2016). Who is eye? An autoethnographic view on higher educational spaces from a Pasifika girl. In e. emerald, R. E. Rinehart, & A. Garcia (Eds.), *Global south ethnographies. Minding the senses* (pp. 199–208). Rotterdam, Netherlands: Sense.

Kincheloe, J., & McLaren, P. (2002). Rethinking critical theory and qualitative research. In Y. Zou & E. Trueba (Eds.), *Ethnography and schools: Qualitative approaches to the study of education* (pp. 87–138). Lanham, MD: Rowman & Littlefield Publishers.

Pihama, L. (1993). *Tungia te ururua, kia tupu whakaritorito te tupu o te harakeke: A critical analysis of parents as first teachers.* Unpublished master's thesis, The University of Auckland.

Smith, L. T. (1999). *Decolonizing methodologies: Research and indigenous peoples.* London & New York: Zed Books.

Young, L. (1990). *Justice and the politics of difference.* Princeton, NJ: Princeton University Press.

SOCIALLY CRITICAL PERSPECTIVES—
HISTORY AND CONCEPTS

# Chapter 6  Critical awakening: Teaching and learning a politicised world

Jennifer Tatebe

*School of Critical Studies in Education*
*Faculty of Education and Social Work*
*The University of Auckland*

**Abstract**

Our preservice teachers often lament that the politics and philosophy of education are not relevant to them, citing their goal of "just wanting to be teachers." The purpose of this chapter is to introduce critical theory to an audience of educators. The chapter begins with a historical overview of the development of the philosophical tradition of social critical theory from its conception by the Frankfurt scholars in the early 20th century. Building upon its traditional roots, the chapter moves towards exploring the development of critical theory as a process of social analysis and critique. Five key elements of critical theory are explored and applied to educational contexts demonstrating a relationship between theory and education (Apple, 1979). In response to growing inequities in society and schools, this chapter positions critical theory as a fundamental means of connecting education, and the practices of teaching and learning, to social, economic, and political life.

**Key words**
Critical theory—social justice—privilege—disadvantage

## *Introduction*

The New Zealand education system promotes the value of inclusivity. The concept of creating a learning environment where "all" students experience academic success by building the "skills and knowledge for work and life" enabling them to participate in society, is embedded in educational policy (Ministry of Education, 2014, 2016b). Disparities in achievement clearly signal how the current education system does not serve all students equally, despite these strong altruistic goals. The Ministry of Education has identified four priority learner groups: Māori students, Pasifika students, learners with special education needs, and students from low socioeconomic backgrounds (Ministry of Education, 2016a). A holistic approach to understanding how to meet the needs of these particular groups of learners requires teachers to have knowledge of the origins, challenges, and outcomes of the wider societal inequities that create educational inequities. The application of critical theory to educational concerns offers a theoretical foundation from which to explain how schools are social institutions, which reflect and contribute to maintaining the inequities visible in schools.

## *Historical origins*

The origins of critical theory are generally attributed to the Frankfurt School, comprised of a group of German social scientists who established the Institute for Social Research in 1923. The Frankfurt scholars, as they were known, had intellectual roots in Marxism, philosophy, psychology, and sociology. The work of Karl Marx was a signfiicant influence on the Frankfurt scholars. Marx emphasised the inequities between the dominant, wealthy bourgeoisie ruling class and the working class proletariat. Unifying the Frankfurt scholars from across the range of disciplines was their aim of examining and critiquing the contemporary tensions between the realities of society and the existing belief systems. As Giroux (1984) explains, the dominant forces of capitalism are a key example of the ideologies the critical scholars sought to challenge and critique. The Frankfurt scholars ultimately sought to generate transformative social change.

## What is critical theory?

Critical theory is fundamentally a "school of thought and process of critique" (Giroux, 1984, p. 8). In the critical tradition, "critique" refers to a deep engagement and analysis of structures, policies, and practices that illuminate underlying societal inequities. Young (1990) discusses the process of critique as "normative reflection", which acknowledges the unique historical and social context of societal ideals, norms, and tensions. Knowledge and facts are therefore socially constructed, reflecting the power dynamics of multiple social and historical contexts in which they are located. Kincheloe and McLaren (2002) define critical theory as a form of inquiry "concerned in particular with issues of power and justice and the ways that the economy; matters of race, class, and gender; ideologies; discourses; education; relation and other social institutions, and cultural dynamics, interact to construct a social system" (p. 90). Methods of inquiry to explore social issues, problems and tensions require deeper examination of several key elements described in the following section.

In this chapter, the term critical theory is employed to refer to scholarship that is underpinned by critical analysis and reflection on social, economic, and political systems with the intention of bringing about transformative change. A brief discussion of theory offers a conceptual starting point from which to examine critical social theory as a philosophical tradition. Theory, as presented in this chapter aligns with Anyon's visual representation of an "architecture of ideas" or "a coherent structure of interrelated concepts" (Anyon, 2009, p. 3). Theory, therefore, allows for deeper examination of phenomena and enhanced explanatory power. Theory, however, is not precluded from interpretation. In acknowledging the subjective use of theory, Anyon signals how even well-intentioned use of theory can be used to maintain or challenge existing social systems. In the discussion that follows, I articulate my interpretation of critical theory.

## Characteristics of critical theory

This section of the chapter presents five key elements or characteristics of critical theory that are central to the examination of core issues and tensions in society. They are: power, politics, enlightenment, emancipation, and empowerment. Each term will be explained separately with use of examples to illustrate how they operate in our society. A final example will demonstrate how multiple key characteristics are intertwined with social issues.

### Power

Within the context of critical theory, power is a ubiquitous yet complex concept. Power operates at different levels. For instance, individuals and groups may hold economic, political, and/or social power. Critical theorists have a particular interest in the ways in which power is unequally distributed amongst individuals, groups, and society at large. Power, in this sense, is often discussed through terms such as "domination" and "subordination." Those holding the most economic, political, or social power are in the dominant position while those with less power are, by definition, part of the subordinate group. Power can therefore be described as a relational concept in that it is based on the relationship between individuals or groups with more power over those with less power or influence.

### Politics

The phrase "everything is political" is a common expression. The definition employed in this chapter draws on the scholarship of Iris Marion Young. Young (1990) describes politics as institutional arrangements that are subject to collective decision making. Various levels of local and national governments, which create laws and regulations to govern society, are prime examples. Cultural and social practices, however, are examples of more informal institutional arrangements that guide societies. In New Zealand, culturally relevant greeting practices guide the way individuals and groups are introduced and welcomed in private and social settings. Reflecting New Zealand's bicultural heritage, introductions (at school) may include handshakes or a hongi (a Māori greeting involving pressing one's nose and forehead to those of another person). Inclusion of bicultural practices in schools in New Zealand is inherently political, sending clear signals about the ways in which social and cultural practices hold the potential to influence collective decision making that governs our schools and society.

### *Enlightenment*

Enlightenment refers to the process of "raising the consciousness" of the marginalised and oppressed. This definition of enlightenment is based on two premises: that the world is composed of contested, and often competing, ideas; and that society is therefore a site of struggle. Enlightenment occurs through the questioning and analysis of contested social conditions leading to greater awareness and understanding by those who are marginalised and oppressed. Scholars such as Kincheloe and McLaren discuss the dialogic nature of the "social construction of experience" (Kincheloe & McLaren, 2002, p. 88). This new knowledge or enlightenment assists in explaining the social conditions that can lead to their empowerment and ultimately transformation of an unequal social order.

### *Empowerment*

Empowerment is a natural extension of enlightenment. It is often discussed as an extension of participation; however, the definition in this chapter aligns with scholarship that underscores the *quality* of participation in decision making and processes (Oxaal & Baden, 1997). Empowerment also describes the transitional process of marginalised individuals' and groups' increasing control and power within their existing, and often unequal, social conditions. Empowerment occurs at multiple levels. At the individual level, the aim is to improve one's own quality of life by acting as an agent of change through active participation in democratic processes. Community empowerment occurs when individuals work collectively to bring new social meaning and change to their social conditions. Individuals draw on personal knowledge and contribute through their social and professional networks to initiate change at wider structural or institutional levels. Individual and community empowerment seeks to create a more equal and democratic society.

### *Emancipation*

Emancipation is closely linked to empowerment. Emancipation refers broadly to the liberation from domination and oppression. Steinberg and Kincheloe (2010) describe emancipation as the process of seeking control of one's life within a "justice-oriented community" through examining the social, economic, and political contextual factors that influence individuals' and groups' ability to make decisions about their lives (p. 143). Steinberg and Kincheloe are careful to acknowledge the complexity and range of emancipatory interests that may be individual and collective; and span or cut across social, economic, historical, and political interests. The authors also note the conceptual limitations of emancipation by acknowledging critics who argue that we can never be completely free of the sociopolitical contexts in which we live. Emancipation, regardless, aligns with critical theory's main aim to "disrupt, to challenge, and to promote moral action" (p. 149). Justice and social justice are often associated with critical theory. So, what do we mean by social justice? The discussion of social justice that follows examines three prevalent perspectives.

## *Definition of social justice*

Conceptions of social justice are abundant. This chapter explores three of its perspectives. The first is the dominant "distributive model" paradigm. Philosopher John Rawls' Principles of Justice exemplify the distributive view of justice. Rawls describes social justice as the "basic structure of society" or the ways in which "major social institutions [being political constitution, as well as economic and social arrangements] distribute fundamental rights and duties and determine the division of advantage from social cooperation" (Rawls, 1999, p. 4). A Rawlsian view of social justice, representative of the distributive model, argues for a more "fair" or equitable distribution of social and economic resources, and democratic rights and participation.

Nancy Fraser builds on Rawls' justice-as-fairness argument. Fraser's social justice model is built upon the concepts of redistribution, recognition, and representation. Posited as the "politics of redistribution", Fraser extends the definition of redistribution from solely a socio-economic or a class-based concept to one that is "collective" or that acknowledges the intersection of socioeconomic injustice with gender, sexuality, and ethnicity (Fraser, 1995). Recognition refers to the acknowledgement of difference such as diverse identities and experiences. Justice through recognition occurs through the recognition of marginalised groups through greater inclusion and participation in dominant social practices. Fraser's social justice framework has been extended to include a third dimension of "representation" (Fraser, 2007, 2008). The concept of representation is political in its reference to membership, social belonging, and inclusion in social and political life. It also refers to the process of participating in the decision-making processes. Fraser's social justice framework is useful in exploring the increasingly complexity of social justice claims that cut across economic, social, and political axes.

Iris Marion Young presents a third social justice paradigm. Her critique of distributive social justice models has led to the development of a "social relational" framework. Young's (1990) critique of the distributive model highlights its limited consideration of social structure and "institutional context". In contrast, she argues for greater emphasis on social structures, or the relationships between people in society and their social positions, which can influence social justice claims. As Young explains, institutional context includes structures, practices, rules, norms, language, and symbols that operate within the state, family, civil society, and the workplace. She argues that greater emphasis should be placed on non-distributive topics such as "decision making structures and procedures, division of labor, and culture" (p. 22). Young, therefore, views social justice as the "elimination of institutionalized domination and oppression" (p. 15). Domination, according to Young, refers to institutional constraints that prevent individuals from participating in the processes of self-determination.

Similar to Young, Apple (1979) describes structural or institutional phenomena as "the basic ways institutions, people, and modes of production, distribution and consumption are organized and controlled [and] dominate cultural life" (p. 2). Meanwhile, Young defines oppression as the "institutional constraint on self-development" (Young, 1990, p. 37). Institutions may include governments and political parties, religious groups, universities, and social groups and clubs, amongst others. These institutions operate within a system of laws and regulations and are, therefore, forms of oppression. These political, social and economic institutions define and divide society into dominant and marginalised social groups. For example, in New Zealand, as elsewhere around the world, political parties serve to categorise citizens along political and often social, economic, and cultural lines.

## Social justice in education

In education, the term "social justice" is equally debated. Gorski (2013) critiques the use of social justice as a "stand in" for diversity. His critique of this practice is two-fold. First, social justice is being used as a "catch all" phrase for all strands of diversity (sexuality, gender, disability, etc.). Secondly, Gorski explains his concern that the embracement of social justice in education reflects a shift in language that has not equally transferred to institutional change and actions to address inequities in schools and society. Acknowledging Gorski's arguments, I refer to two definitions that reflect current thinking about social justice in education. The first is Bell's (2013) explanation of social justice which draws on Fraser's concept of representation discussed in the previous section. Bell (2013) presents social justice as the "equal participation of all groups in society that is mutually shaped to meet their needs" (p. 21).

Democracy and self-determination are also central features of this equity of participation perspective of social justice. Full participation in society has historically been set within a human rights discourse, particularly in the American context. Grant and Gibson (2013) trace the origins of social justice to fundamental civil, political, economic, and social human rights which they summarise as "the protection of both individual liberties and economic security" (p. 88). Discussions of social justice in education also emphasise the concept of equity of opportunity. Often discussed as the "opportunity gap," a growing number of educational scholars identify unequal access to educational and life opportunities as a key reason for inequities in educational outcomes (Darling-Hammond, 2010; Ladson-Billings 2013).

The discussion of social justice in education concludes this first half of the chapter. With a historical overview of the development of critical theory, a definition, and five key characteristics of the critical philosophical tradition now outlined, the second half of the chapter explores the application of critical theory in education.

## Critical theory and education

One of the challenges of teaching the philosophy of education is to convey its value and application to the profession of teaching. Initially our preservice teachers often find it challenging to see critical theory's connections to the everyday complexities of school and classroom life.

Consequently, some preservice teachers consistently question the relevance of critical theory to their work as teachers. In other words, they question the value of critical theory to and within education. A response to this important question draws on a variety of critical scholarship.

Anyon (2009) presents critical theory as an "architecture of ideas" or set of concepts that help to understand and explain phenomena and unpack how social systems function (p. 3). By examining contextual complexities, critical theory provides a framework from which to improve on existing understanding of the given phenomena. For example, she explains how "powerful interest groups, political or business elites, or individual officials and politicians exert their influence through laws, regulatory mandates, access to the print and television media, and influence on the policies of institutions" (p. 13). With this statement, Anyon advances two important points: critical theory's ability to act as the bridge between what occurs in and outside of schools; and how understanding the wider political, social and economic contexts in which schools are located provides deeper meaning to the education system.

When asked why preservice teachers must learn about critical theory as part of a philosophy of education course, I offer these three responses:

1. Critical theory is a means of untangling the social, economic, and political processes that create inequities and injustices in education and wider society.
2. A critical theoretical analysis is a comprehensive explanation of everyday phenomena in schools and society.
3. Critical theory is a vehicle that illuminates gaps and silences in the dominant narratives and existing understandings of concepts and knowledge. Engaging with critical theory assists us to move beyond initial perspectives and encourages us to see things from a different point of view.

Gibson (1986) concisely summarises the application of critical theory to education as: the identification of inequities in education; the educational processes that enable the inequities to occur and persist; and concludes with proposing solutions to the identified inequities. Building on Gibson's three-fold approach, I argue that critical theory makes another valuable contribution—it makes educational concerns relevant to those in fields outside of education.

I have outlined the origins and key characteristics of critical theory, examined multiple perspectives of social justice, and made arguments in support of the value of critical theory's application to education. In the final section of the chapter I offer an example of critical theory's potential to deepen preservice teachers' understanding of educational inequities present in schools across New Zealand. I have chosen to focus broadly on the ways in which privilege and disadvantage operate in an educational text. My analysis moves from a macropolitical or structural level, to a mesopolitical or school-based sphere of influence, and concludes with examining how teachers at the micropolitical level may encounter privilege and disadvantage in everyday classroom interactions.

## Confronting privilege and disadvantage in Aotearoa New Zealand

In this section I focus on income and wealth inequality while acknowledging the important contributions of scholars who explore inequality through ethnic, cultural, gender, and other lenses. Similarly, I recognise and appreciate the multiple ways these issues of identity intersect and can be examined from various economic, social, and political perspectives. Having made these acknowledgements, I unequivocally argue that income and wealth inequality are two of the most critical concerns in New Zealand. Of course, inequality is not a uniquely New Zealand issue; a wealth of cross-disciplinary data illustrate how countries around the world are also experiencing a similar growing gap between rich and poor (OECD, 2015).

### Macropolitics and education

Encouraging signs of greater public awareness about income and wealth inequality have emerged from recent media attention, as well as targeted research across multiple fields (Child Poverty Action Group, 2008; Rashbrooke, 2013). Research provides knowledge of rising inequality, yet the outcomes of poverty are readily visible in many communities. Discomforting stories of families living in cars, unable to afford rent, and struggling to provide adequate food and clothing for their children are now part of a recurring narrative about the socioeconomic climate in New Zealand. At a macropolitical, or structural, level, critical theory opens possibilities for our future teachers to critique and make sense of the ways in which inequality is the outcome of social and economic policies. For example, as discussed in other chapters the introduction of neoliberal values and free market economic policies in the 1980s contributed to increasing income and wealth inequality (Humpage, 2017).

Neoliberal politics led to the scaling back of once-strong New Zealand social policies in housing, the benefit system, and pensions amongst others (once known as the "welfare state") which in turn led to one of the largest rises in inequality in the world. The reality for middle- and lower-income families was, and continues to be, an increasingly uncomfortable and uncertain situation. A macropolitical analysis across major sectors including health, justice, social development, foreign affairs, and trade allows for preservice teachers to begin to understand how social and economic policies in other sectors directly influence educational policy and everyday experiences in schools.

Widening gaps in income, for example, create a snowball effect on the housing and education sectors. National census data indicates that the top 2% of New Zealanders earn $150,000 or more per annum. Also, the top 1% of New Zealanders have seen their incomes consistently rise by 7% to 9% since the 1990s (Perry, 2016). Meanwhile, the bottom 30% of New Zealanders earn less than $30,000 (Statistics New Zealand, 2014). The effects have been sharply felt in the housing market. Housing prices across the country have been on the rise with average Auckland house prices reaching an unprecedented $1m. Income and housing are critical to understanding educational inequities due to their current inclusion in two educational policies: the decile system and school zoning practices. The decile system is New Zealand's controversial educational funding scheme. The decile system draws on national census data to generate an *approximate* socioeconomic "snapshot" of each school's local community (Ministry of Education, 2016c). Income is one of five factors included in the calculation; however, decile calculations only measure and reflect household incomes that fall in the lowest 20% nationally.

School decile ratings determine school funding that influences all aspects of a school's everyday operations. Schools with decile ratings of

1–3 receive additional funding intended to assist with the overcoming some of the challenges of lower socioeconomic communities. Although developed with good intentions as a means of addressing educational inequities, the decile system has become the subject of intense critique due to its misuse as proxies for teacher, school, and student quality (Thrupp, 2009). To be clear, school decile ratings are a blunt measure of the socioeconomic demographics of a school's local community. Decile ratings do not provide any information about student achievement, or the quality of teachers and schools. Incomes and housing are also central factors in school zoning policies. At the time of writing this chapter, the outgoing Minister of Education had clearly signalled her intention of phasing out the decile system; however, with the election of a new Government, it remains unknown what, if any, changes to educational funding will occur.

Zoning is another educational policy with direct links to the decile system. In New Zealand, each school may set a zone or catchment area for enrolment purposes. Living within the school zone guarantees a place at that particular school. Those living outside a set zone are able to apply for an out-of-zone placement, if space is available. By definition, income and housing are fundamental criteria for attending a desired school. Real estate "for sale" signs are excellent examples of the relationship between income, housing, and schooling in New Zealand. For example, these signs often include descriptions of their placement in desirable school zones which, in turn, influence house sale prices. Critical theory permits us to look past initial surface-level impressions of what goes on in education through analysis of wider social, economic, and political contexts in which schools and the teaching profession are located.

## Mesopolitics and education

As Anyon (2009) suggests, public policies are educational policies. At the school or mesopolitical level, critical theory opens up possibilities for understanding how social and economic policies have a direct influence on teaching and learning practices. The following quote from a preservice teacher's reflection on teaching in a low-decile school (1–3 school decile ranking) provides a basis from which to examine the power of a critical theoretical analysis of a challenge of teaching in a disadvantaged school context. She writes:

> While some parents will be concerned and supportive, I believe that many do not have their children's' best interest at heart. If they did, they would find out about the importance of breakfast, of books at home, of reading to their children, of backing up the school over discipline issues etc. (Tatebe, 2014, p. 155)

In absence of critical theory, it may appear as if some parents' limited involvement and support of their child's education is a "choice." In comparison, critical theory permits a deeper examination of social and school factors that offers an alternative view of this commentary. Refering to the five key characteristics of critical theory and an understanding of social justice as discussed in the first half of the chapter, a critical perspective would assist this preservice teacher to connect economic policies to disparities in income that can lead to the absence of children's breakfast and books, as well as available time for parents to support children's learning at home. Similarly, an analysis of power and politics would likely reveal potential cultural differences in ideas about discipline, and parenting techniques. Thus critical theory illuminates what may initially seem to be *school* concerns, as outcomes of broader economic and social policies.

### *Micropolitics and education*

Micropolitics refers to the everyday teaching and learning practices of our educators. With an introduction to critical theory, we now shift to what I refer to as the "so what?" question. More specifically, what *are* the implications of engaging with critical theory for our preservice teachers? One hope is that preservice teachers will gain greater awareness of how education, and teaching and learning, are directly influenced by wider social and economic policies. As Welner and Carter (2013) suggest, this view shifts our attention away from deficit theorising, or the "deficiencies in the foundational components of societies, schools, and communities that produce significant differences in educational—and ultimately socioeconomic—outcomes" (p. 3). Instead, education may be viewed as a reflection of society. A second hope is that some preservice teachers may move from this heightened state of awareness towards taking individual measures to address the educational inequities they encounter in their classrooms and schools. It is with great excitement that some preservice teachers awaken to a world of new possibilities as the result of engaging with a critical perspective. These preservice teachers often ask what they can do as individuals. To this I refer to the work of Michael Apple (2013) who offers three tangible responses. Apple suggests that the work of critical scholars is to examine societal inequities; to identify spaces and possibilities to confront such inequities; and to support individuals and groups committed to taking actions to address the challenges associated with addressing them.

## Conclusion

Preservice teachers who express interest in critical theory often ask the difficult question of how they can engage in socially critical teaching pedagogy. It is challenging to provide concrete responses. Acknowledging the complexities of power relations, external and internal to education, and unique teaching contexts, each individual teacher is best placed to find creative opportunities to address educational inequities. Responses may be curricular, pedagogical, or community-based. For those seeking a firm example, I suggest an on-going commitment to engaging in socially critical educational scholarship that examines inequities in schools.

## References

Apple, M. (1979). On analyzing hegemony. In M. Apple (Ed.), *Ideology and curriculum* (pp. 1–25). London, UK: Routledge & Kegan Paul.

Apple, M. W. (2013). *Can education change society?* New York, NY: Routledge.

Anyon, J. (2009). Critical social theory, educational research, and intellectual agency. In J. Anyon (Ed.), *Theory and educational research: Toward critical social explanation* (pp. 1–23). New York, NY: Routledge.

Bell, L. A. (2013). What is social justice? In M. Adams, W. Blumenfeld, C. Castaneda, H. W. Hackman, M. L. Peters, & X. Zuniga (Eds.), *Readings for diversity and social justice* (3rd ed., pp. 21–26). New York, NY: Routledge Taylor & Francis Group.

Child Poverty Action Group. (2008). *Left behind: How social and income inequalities damage New Zealand children.* Auckland: Author.

Darling-Hammond, L. (2010). *The flat world and education: How America's commitment to equity will determine our future*. New York, NY: Teachers College Press.

Fraser, N. (1995). From redistribution to recognition? Dilemmas of justice in a "postsocialist" age. *New Left Review, 212*, 68–93.

Fraser, N. (2007). Re-framing justice in a globalizing world. In T. Lovell (Ed.), *(Mis)recognition, social inequality and social justice: Nancy Fraser and Pierre Bourdieu* (pp. 17–35). London, UK: Routledge.

Fraser, N. (2008). *Scales of justice: Reimagining political space in a globalizing world*. Cambridge, UK: Polity Press.

Gibson, R. (1986). Critical theory and education. *Critical theory and education* (pp. 44–65; 3). London: Hodder and Stoughton.

Giroux, H. (1984). *Critical theory and educational practice*. Melbourne, VIC: Deakin University Press.

Gorski, P. (2013, February 19). Social justice: Not just another term for "diversity." Retrieved from https://acpacsje.wordpress.com/2013/02/19/social-justice-not-just-another-term-for-diversity-by-paul-c-gorski/

Grant, C. A., & Gibson, M. L. (2013). "The path of social justice": A human rights history of social justice education. *Equity & Excellence in Education, 46*(1), 81–99. doi:10.1080/10665684.2012.750190

Humpage, L. (2017). The land of me and money? New Zealand society under neoliberalism. In A. Bell, V. Elizabeth, T. McIntosh, & M. Wynyard (Eds.), *Land of milk and honey?: Making sense of Aotearoa New Zealand* (pp. 121–133). Auckland: Auckland University Press.

Kincheloe, J., & McLaren, P. (2002). Rethinking critical theory and qualitative research. In Y. Zou, & E. Trueba (Eds.), *Ethnography and schools: Qualitative approaches to the study of education* (pp. 87–138). Lanham, MD: Rowman & Littlefield Publishers.

Ladson-Billings, G. (2013). Lack of achievement or loss of opportunity? In P. Carter, & K. Welner (Eds.), *Closing the opportunity gap: What America must do to give all children an even chance* (pp. 11–22). New York, NY: Oxford University Press.

Ministry of Education. (2014). *Investing in educational success: Working group report*. Wellington: Author.

Ministry of Education. (2016a). *Annual report 2016*. Wellington: Author.

Ministry of Education. (2016b). *Four year plan 2016–2020*. Wellington: Author.

Ministry of Education. (2016c, 29 November). *School deciles*. Retrieved from http://www.education.govt.nz/school/running-a-school/resourcing/operational-funding/school-decile-ratings/

OECD. (2015). *In it together: Why less inequality benefits all*. Pais. France: OECD Publishing. doi:10.1787/9789264235120-en

Oxaal, Z., & Baden, S. (1997). *Gender and empowerment: Definitions, approaches and implications for policy*. Brighton, UK: Bridge Institute of Development Studies, University of Sussex.

Perry, B. (2016). *Household incomes in New Zealand: Trends in indicators of inequality and hardship 1982–2015*. Wellington: Ministry of Social Development. Retrieved from https://www.msd.govt.nz/about-msd-and-our-work/publications-resources/monitoring/household-incomes/

Rashbrooke, M. (Ed.). (2013). *Inequality: A New Zealand crisis*. Wellington: Bridget Williams Books.

Rawls, J. (1999). *A theory of justice* (Revised Ed.). Cambridge, MA: Belknap Press.

Statistics New Zealand. (2014). *2013 census QuickStats about income*. Wellington: Author.

Steinberg, S. R., & Kincheloe, J. L. (2010). Power, emancipation, and complexity: Employing critical theory. *Power and Education, 2*(2), 140–151. doi:10.2304/power.2010.2.2.140

Tatebe, J. (2014). *The politics of discomfort: Unsettling conversations about preservice teachers' engagement with socioeconomic disadvantage*. Unpublished doctoral thesis, The University of Auckland.

Thrupp, M. (2009). High visibility: More clarity needed in arguments over deciles. *New Zealand Education Review, 14*(5), 6–7.

Welner, K., & Carter, P. (2013). Achievement gaps arise from opportunity gaps. In P. Carter, & K. Welner (Eds.), *Closing the opportunity gap: What America must do to give all children an even chance* (pp. 1–10). New York, NY: Oxford University Press.

Young, I. (1990). *Justice and the politics of difference*. Princeton, NJ: Princeton University Press.

THINKING ABOUT SOCIALLY CRITICAL
PERSPECTIVES IN TODAY'S WORLD

# Chapter 7  Kaupapa Māori: Decolonising politics and philosophy in education

Mera Lee-Penehira

*Te Puna Wānanga*
*Faculty of Education and Social Work*
*University of Auckland*

**Abstract**

Kaupapa Māori is a philosophical framework that centres and privileges Māori ways of being, knowing and thinking in education and research paradigms (Penehira, 2011; Smith, L.T., 2007). Despite kaupapa Māori now being a well-recognised theoretical and methodological approach in education in Aotearoa, the inclusion of Māori philosophers and broader Indigenous politics in teacher education remains minimal. Researchers and educators alike have a torrid history of using research and education spaces for the further oppression of Indigenous peoples (Mead, 1994; Penehira, Smith, Green & Aspin, 2011; Pihama, 2001). For many generations, non-Indigenous researchers have entered our communities to glean information, collect data, and then apply analyses devoid of Indigenous ways of knowing and behaving (Kidman, 2007; Smith, L.T., 2007). The end results have not produced good education outcomes for Māori. Linda Tuhiwai Smith (1997), whose work centres largely on decolonising research methodologies in education, provides significant guidance to both kaupapa Māori research and education. Teacher educators and academics play a significant role in the continued development of research ideologies and methodologies that ensure the safety and respect of Māori, Native and Indigenous students and educators. Drawing largely on the author's doctoral study (Penehira, 2011), this chapter encourages progressive change, ultimately aimed at greater recognition of Māori and Indigenous philosophies, and decolonising the academy in the context of teacher education.

**Key words**
Kaupapa Māori—colonisation—Indigenous—mana kaitiakitanga

## *Introduction*

The continued colonial dominance of non-Māori and non-Indigenous ways of being and knowing and, of course, teaching in the academy, has been a shared and growing concern amongst Indigenous and non-Indigenous academics alike in recent decades (Battiste, Bell, & Findlay, 2002; May & Hill, 2005; L. T. Smith, 1997; Pihama, 2001; Walker, 2003). The genesis for this chapter was in the author's experience of integrating kaupapa Māori into an English-medium politics and philosophy course in teacher education at The University of Auckland. There is an intention here to both recognise the current shortcomings of the academy in terms of decolonising our teaching, and to encourage progressive change, ultimately aimed at greater recognition of Māori and Indigenous philosophies. Drawing on the author's own doctoral study (Penehira, 2011), in the first section of the chapter, kaupapa Māori is presented as a philosophy in its own right. This is followed by the more detailed framework, mana kaitiakitanga, which provides a greater depth of understanding to the philosophy of kaupapa Māori. The chapter concludes with a discussion of ways forward taking us beyond the colonial constraints of education.

## Colonisation and kaupapa Māori

Academics have a shameful history of using education as a tool for the further oppression of Indigenous peoples (Lee, 2009; Mead, 1994; Pihama, 2001; Simons & Smith, 1998). For many generations, non-Indigenous teachers and academics have entered our communities to teach us things that would assist in our initial and continued assimilation into what became a colonised land of Aotearoa (New Zealand). The measurement and analysis of our academic progress has been determined in ways that are devoid of Indigenous ways of knowing and behaving (Kidman, 2007; L. T. Smith, 2007). The end result has been to continue to teach de-contextualised ways that barely address cultural ways of being and knowing, and which have a long way to go before meeting the needs of Māori and other Indigenous students in the academy. We have continued to teach politics and philosophy in ways that, although improving, might still position Indigenous peoples as victims of their own wrongdoing; thus, justifying the continued role of the coloniser to teach us the *right way*, their way, in order to save ourselves from our own destruction.

Colonisation is a process whereby Indigenous peoples are systematically taught to do things according to the colonisers' view of the world (C. W. Smith, 2002; G. H. Smith, 1997; Pihama, 1993). In so doing, Indigenous ways of knowing and behaving are lost. Worse, they may no longer be deemed as of any importance whatsoever. These are experiences that are shared amongst Indigenous peoples from many lands. It is these shared experiences that "Indigenous communities associate with racism, with inequality and injustices" (Bargh, 2007, p. 57).

The analysis presented here is multi-layered and shares commonalities with many other Indigenous writers. These layers include: how colonisation affects one's ability to think and speak; how we view our position in the communities in which we have been raised, and the communities in which we now live; how we view our freedom or our entrapment; and how we view our position in the environments in which we move, i.e., the academic institutions, the business world, the governance institutions, social institutions, sporting institutions. Kaupapa Māori approaches to philosophy include all of these things and more.

It can be argued that the analysis of colonisation is indeed critical to every facet of life, for Māori, Indigenous and non-Indigenous or Pākehā (Aotearoa term for non-Māori and/or non-Indigenous) alike. In the context of this chapter, understanding colonisation in relation to politics, philosophy, education, and the academy is significant. Indigenous peoples have shown both resistance to and resilience against early attempts to keep us in our place as "lowly educated natives". However, many have not. Many of us still suffer from poor educational outcomes. So, what are the key elements that influence our ability to overcome the colonising forces that exist in the academy?

The work of Linda Tuhiwai Smith (1997), whose doctoral studies centred largely on decolonising research methodologies in the context of education, goes some way to answering this question. In order to begin this discussion, it is necessary to consider, firstly, the converse of decolonising methodologies and/or education; that is, "colonising methodologies and/or education". Colonising education may be considered, amongst other things, as that which privileges academic literature and empirical evidence over and above oral accounts (Pihama, 2005; C. W. Smith, 2002; L. T. Smith, 1999). This is not to say that decolonising methodologies and education counter this by privileging oral accounts over academic literature and empirical evidence, however. Rather, it is about giving voice to material previously not recognised as valid in relation to research and academic documentation. This includes, but is not exclusive to, oral accounts. Decolonising methodologies and education also acknowledge, for example, the historical and contemporary narratives contained in traditional carving, song, and performance.

Decolonising education and research seek to unravel data from all sources, including those mentioned above, as well as material from non-Indigenous researchers. It is important to note that it is not the sole intent of kaupapa Māori or other Indigenous approaches in education to counter the education approaches of colonisers, as could be suggested by the term *decolonising education*. Rather, it is about doing what is necessary in order to assist people to become decolonised, to become self-determining, and to be resilient to the forces of colonisation (Bishop, 2008; Durie, 1998; Walters, 2006). Sometimes this results in direct challenges to past research and to non-Indigenous philosophies. However, to solely focus a methodology or philosophical approach on this task would be to fall short of the ultimate aim of self-determination. This aim cannot be achieved by simply deconstructing historical or recent research in education paradigms alone, given the narrow foci of the majority of these works in terms of the dimensions of our lives that it has covered.

Kaupapa Māori research and academic development began largely in the area of education, closely followed by the health sector. Currently, there remains a larger force of kaupapa Māori researchers in both of these areas than in any other. However, with the current drive to increase numbers of Māori graduating with PhDs, we are seeing a greater spread of Māori researchers throughout the various faculties of our universities. Concurrently, we have many researchers emerging from our own whare wānanga (Indigenous universities).

Kaupapa Māori by literal definition is simply: about Māori. Māori is defined in dictionaries as "natural" (Moorefield, 2005). So, it could be argued that kaupapa Māori is about *what is natural* or about *being natural*. The discussion of kaupapa Māori research links and often overlaps with that of kaupapa Māori theory. "Theory" is defined in the online Merriam-Webster dictionary as "an ideal or hypothetical set of facts, principles, or circumstances".[3] Having experiences, and indeed a life, centred on things Māori, gives the *circumstances* and the *principles* by which everyday life routines and events are carried out. It does not, however, feel, in any sense of the word, *hypothetical*. How then does one who practises or lives in a Māori way come to have an understanding of kaupapa Māori theory? I argue that, to develop theory from a lived base of understanding is simply to develop and undertake analyses of those circumstances and principles by which that living is framed. It could be concluded, therefore, that a Māori analysis of things Māori is one manifestation of what kaupapa Māori theory, politics, and philosophy is.

Historically, much social research has centred on "proper research" being considered as such when it is conducted in an impartial or objective way. Kaupapa Māori research, by contrast, actually requires the researcher to situate himself or herself in some way *inside* the research and largely remove levels of objectivity. Being subjective—that is, to

---

3 https://www.merriam-webster.com/dictionary/theory

see oneself as a part of the subject or subject group—is advantageous in kaupapa Māori research because it implies one's accountability to the research group and the research outcomes. Subjectivity is indeed necessary in order for the research to be deemed valid in kaupapa Māori terms. This accountability and responsibility to the people is particularly important in the context of the historical injustices perpetuated by research and education of Indigenous peoples.

The notion of insider–outsider research has differing levels of application. For example, some kaupapa Māori researchers (Royal, 1996; C. W. Smith, 2008) go so far as to state that the researcher should have direct genealogical ties to the group they are researching. The rationale given is threefold. First, it ensures the same level of accountability to the group applies due to the researcher's familial ties. Secondly, the background and contextual knowledge of the research area and people is much more likely to exist within the researcher, because they know and are known to the community. Thirdly, the researcher remains tied to the community beyond the life of the research, and is therefore able to be held accountable for both the research outcomes and the longevity of the impact of these outcomes.

The accountability that comes with familial ties goes beyond the obvious: that the researcher is one of the people and therefore has a stake in, and is to an extent responsible for, outcomes in the community. The tribal nature of Māori communities contains a complex matrix of roles, positions, and responsibilities. Many relationships exist within whānau; tuakana–teina is one such relationship. Tuakana Nepe (1991) writes about tuakana–teina as it relates to her personal knowledge of whānau, hapū, and iwi, and the family relationships she has experienced:

> At my immediate whānau generation level I am teina to my older sisters and tuakana to my younger sister and two younger brothers. This information influences how we interact, in terms of our reciprocal roles and commitments, to one and other. By virtue of our standing as either tuakana or teina to each other these roles and commitments are binding and fixed. (p. 21)

This appears quite straightforward. At an iwi level, however, the complexities are increased:

> At the iwi level my tuakana–teina relationships are complex and are varied in relation to all my great grandparents, siblings, great grandchildren. The important fact to remember is that the tuakana–teina kin relationships are not restricted to immediate whānau of the generation level referred to, but are applicable too at the extended whānau, the hapū, and the iwi levels … these kinship complexities are applicable to all social relationships. (p. 22)

Clearly, the more extended the interactions, the more complex the relationships. In terms of facilitating research this raises interesting issues. How do the interrelationships and whakapapa between different hapū and iwi impact on the tuakana or teina status of the individuals participating in research? How do researchers mediate these relationships? Do they have enough knowledge to determine the status of participants or is that the role of other members of the tribe or family? These questions stem in the main from a methodological focus. For Māori researchers and educators they will be answered in the construction and use of kaupapa Māori methods and frameworks. Other Indigenous researchers have developed and used their own research tools to answer a similar set of questions.

Linda Tuhiwai Smith (1999) introduced the notion of an Indigenous research agenda that, in essence, highlights important contextual issues to be mindful of when conducting Indigenous research. It provides a framework for mediating and traversing the complexities that arise in such research, ultimately aimed at bringing about self-determination in Indigenous communities:

> The Indigenous research agenda is broad in its scope and ambitious in its intent … some things make this agenda very different from the research agenda of large scientific organisations or of various national science research programmes. There are other elements, however, which are similar to any research programme, which connects research to the 'good' of society. The elements that are different can be found in key words such as healing, decolonisation, spiritual, recovery. (p. 117)

The following chart encompasses these concepts and provides a visual representation of the Indigenous research and, indeed, education context. Linda Tuhiwai Smith (1999) presented this chart as a metaphor of ocean tides, with the processes of healing, decolonisation, transformation, and mobilisation being indicative of the four directions of our world: the northern, the eastern, the southern, and the western. The research and educative processes that we engage in need to be mindful of these four processes. That is, from design through to outcomes, and everything in between, an Indigenous academic needs to be aware of the context in which the research and/or education is placed, and more importantly, that the context is ever-changing as with the tides. This entails one considering how the research and/or education aids or impedes the processes of healing, decolonisation, transformation and mobilisation. In this way the research agenda can be viewed as both a framework to guide research and education, and a framework for analysis of any aspect within it.

Figure 7.1 *The Indigenous Research Agenda*

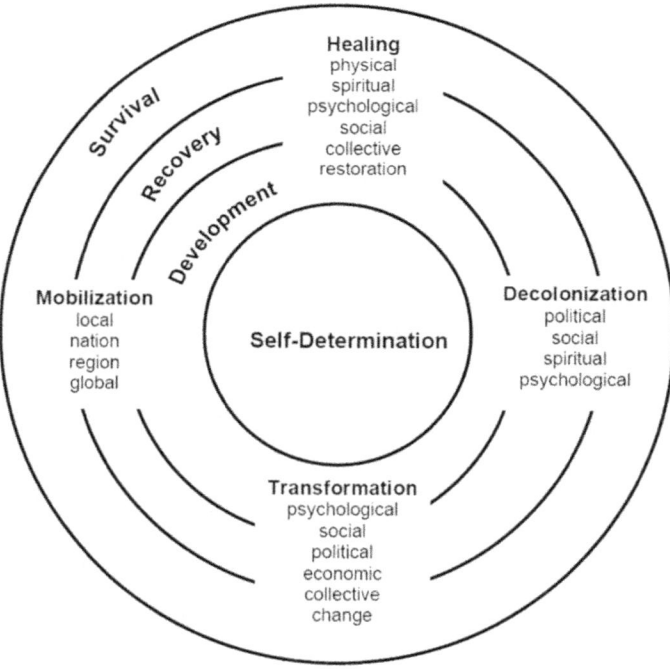

Source: *Decolonizing Methodologies* (p. 117), by L. T. Smith (1999), London, UK and New York, NY: Zed Books. Reprinted with permission.

Contextualising kaupapa Māori alongside the broader Indigenous research and education context is important to decolonising education in Aotearoa New Zealand. Understanding other Indigenous views assists us to better understand our own, and vice versa.

### Mana kaitiakitanga: A kaupapa Māori philosophical framework

This section presents the more detailed framework, mana kaitiakitanga (Penehira, 2011), which provides a greater depth of understanding to the philosophy of kaupapa Māori. Initially developed by Dr Huirangi Waikerepuru, myself, and other students in 1997, mana kaitiakitanga emerged from a series of wānanga (learning institutions) which were ultimately aimed at the resurgence of moko kauwae amongst Taranaki Māori women. It provides an overview of the Māori principle of wellbeing, thus providing an appropriate platform for discussing the intricacies of some aspects of kaupapa Māori as a philosophy.

The framework (see Figure 7.2, following) includes Mouri as one of seven key elements of Māori wellbeing, the other six refer to various aspects of Hau. Mouri and Hau are viewed here as the *carriers* or *indicators* of areas in our lives and in our being that are essential to our wellbeing. This, in the context of the Māori principle of wellbeing, includes physical, spiritual, and emotional states of being. Māori Marsden (1988) describes the relationship between Mouri and Hau, positing that Hau-ora, or the breath of life, is the source from, and by which, Mouri emanates. Whilst saying that, in particular contexts, Hau is used as a synonym for Mouri, Marsden also differentiates between the concepts, advising that Hau is a term only applied to animate life, whereas Mouri can be applied to both animate and inanimate things. He states:

> Mauri was a force or energy mediated by Hauora—the Breath of the Spirit of Life. Mauri Ora was the life-force (mauri) transformed into life-principle by the infusion of life itself. (p. 21)

As shown in the framework below, the seven elements that make up the Māori principle of wellbeing are framed by four further institutions or concepts: health, environment, law and tikanga. In so doing, it is suggested that these institutions engage directly with one's wellbeing and vice versa. That is, the state of health and the environment, the way we operate within the laws and indeed *lores* of our communities, and our knowledge and practice of tikanga, all impact on our wellbeing.

In contrast, our state of wellbeing, or otherwise, impacts on our ability to operate in healthy ways with and within the environment, and to conduct ourselves in law/loreful ways, by knowing and practising tikanga Māori.

The base of the framework includes tapu, tika, pono, hē/hara, and noa. These are concepts which allude to the states of being that we move through and between in everyday life and events. They are significant contributors to the framework, in that these states (or rather our ability to understand what state is necessary for what purpose, and our ability to move between states) are critical to our wellbeing. Whilst a full explanation of these concepts is not essential to achieving the purpose of conveying a sense of understanding of Mouri, the following provides an overview of how these concepts were discussed in the framework development. These concepts can be viewed as a kaupapa Māori philosophical approach, not only to wellbeing, but as indicated in the framework below, to education, environment, health and law. Māori philosophical approaches are necessarily holistic.

Figure 7. 2 *Mana Kaitiakitanga: Māori Principle of Wellbeing Model*

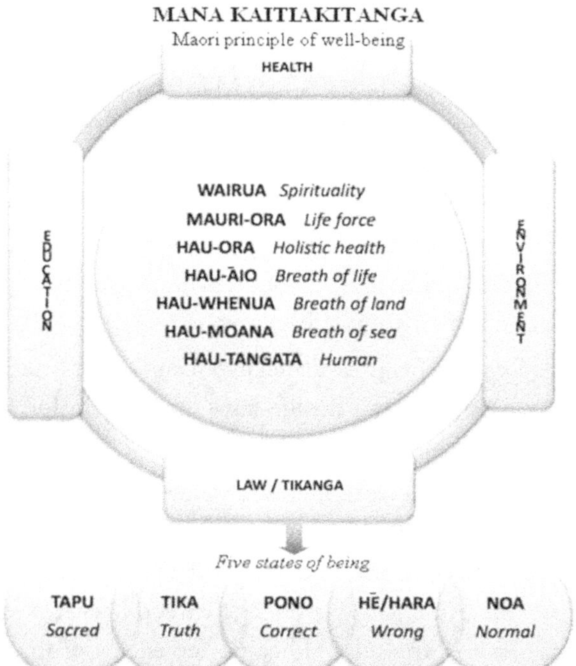

**MANA KAITIAKITANGA**
Maori principle of well-being

HEALTH

EDUCATION

WAIRUA *Spirituality*
MAURI-ORA *Life force*
HAU-ORA *Holistic health*
HAU-ĀIO *Breath of life*
HAU-WHENUA *Breath of land*
HAU-MOANA *Breath of sea*
HAU-TANGATA *Human*

ENVIRONMENT

LAW / TIKANGA

*Five states of being*

| TAPU | TIKA | PONO | HĒ/HARA | NOA |
|---|---|---|---|---|
| Sacred | Truth | Correct | Wrong | Normal |

Source: Penehira, M. (2011), p. 41.

*Tapu* (Sacred): A necessary state of being in order to enable certain things to be achieved or events to be conducted. To gain in-depth understanding of karakia and other forms of traditional knowledge, or to participate in events such as tangihanga, one enters into a state and space of sacredness.

*Tika* (Correct): It is necessary to be able to conduct oneself correctly according to whatever situation, event, or level of thought one is engaged in. This requires an understanding of what is correct in the first instance. In terms of children developing into adults with a healthy sense of wellbeing, it is important that they develop a knowledge and understanding of what is correct. This may be whānau-, hapū- and iwi-specific.

*Pono* (Truth): To operate in a truthful sense enables one to be open to new learning. The relationship between truth and new knowledge is significant, in that our belief is that, if one does not engage truthfully in a learning situation or wānanga, they will not reap the benefits of that situation—they are not in a state to receive, or understand, new knowledge. When one operates from a space other than the truth, it impacts negatively on their wellbeing.

*Hē/hara* (Wrong): In learning, in living and in being well, mistakes are made. This concept recognises that, and its place in the framework reminds us that it is a state that we will all be in from time to time. Being in that state generally detracts from our wellbeing. However, it is significant to understanding the Māori principle of wellbeing that we take new knowledge and understanding from our mistakes; from our time in the state of hē.

*Noa* (Normal): This is the state in which we operate for much of our daily lives, activities, and events. It is well known to us. It is perceived to be the opposite to tapu and provides the basis from which we can enter into other ways of being.

So, if each of these states has a significant place in our lives and, if collectively they provide the basis for the Māori principle of wellbeing, how is it that we move through and between these states? The mediating mechanism—the mechanism that guides us into, through, and out of these states—is simply karakia (prayer or incantation).

We have karakia that specifically take us into a state of tapu for example, and karakia that release us from that tapu. There are karakia that can be used to remind us of what is true and correct (pono and tika), and karakia that caution us about being in the state of hē (wrong). Karakia kai or food blessings are perhaps the most common form of karakia for the state of noa (normal). With an understanding of karakia as the mediating agent of these states of being, it is acknowledged that karakia play a significant role in the Māori principle of wellbeing.

The seven elements of the Māori principle of wellbeing are explained below in the terms and understanding that were applied during the framework development:

*Wairua* (Spirituality): Ngā wai e rua (the two waters) is discussed by Dr Waikerepuru (Personal communication, September 10, 2009) as one interpretation of the concept of wairua. In doing so, he speaks of the spiritual essence emerging from the two fluid sources present at the conception of a child. This can relate also to that which is created when Ranginui and Papatūānuku merged. In terms of how wairua influences the Māori principle of wellbeing, it is essential that one has a connectedness with Indigenously Māori spirituality. That includes knowledge, understanding and practical application of karakia, pure (specific incantation), and waiata.

*Mouri Ora* (Life Force): Refers to the innate life force within each of us. For our wellbeing, it asks us to give consideration to the wellness of our energy, of the force/s that activate us to do things and to operate and interact with our world. This explanation relates to the discussions in development of the mana kaitiakitanga framework and, as the focus of this chapter, this concept is discussed more fully further on.

*Hau Ora* (Holistic Health): Māori conceptualisation of health is holistic, including reference to physical, emotional, and spiritual wellbeing. Hau ora literally may be translated to be breath of life.

*Hau Āio* (Breath of Life): Refers to te hau a Io, or the breath of Io who is recognised by Māori as the supreme being from whom creation is derived.

*Hau Whenua:* (Breath of Land) The wellbeing of humans relating to the wellbeing of the land. Hau Whenua also refers to the relationship between people and the land. If each of these is well (the people and the land), and the relationship between them is active and well, this has a significant positive contribution to Hau Ora. This element also facilitates the notion of tangata whenua, which recognises Māori as people of the land.

*Hau Moana* (Breath of Sea): Similar to Hau Whenua, the wellbeing of humans relating to the wellbeing of the ocean environment. The relationship between people and the ocean is referenced here. The independent wellness of each (the people and the ocean environment) is important, as is the wellness of the interactions between them.

*Hau Tangata:* (Breath of Humanity): Refers to the unique human spirit within each of us. It speaks of both the individual and the collective wellbeing of humanity. Just as Hau Whenua and Hau Moana are about people and their relationship to the land and ocean environments, Hau Tangata is about people and their relationships to, and with, each other. Our wellness as individuals impacts on our ability to relate to, and engage with, others, either enabling us to contribute to, or detract from, the wellness of others and the collective.

As shown here, mouri is but one of seven key elements of the Māori principle of wellbeing. The descriptions of each of these elements allude to what may be perceived as a Māori view of the overlapping nature of aspects of wellbeing. I suggest that, because of this overlapping, there is a strong interdependence between each of these notions. This further suggests that, if just one of the elements is less than well, then all will be affected. The mana kaitiakitanga framework is therefore a holistic one, which provides a platform for understanding the place of mouri in Māori health and wellbeing. Furthermore, mana kaitiakitanga can in fact be viewed as a kaupapa Māori philosophical framework.

## *Moving beyond colonial constraints*

In 2015, I was invited to teach the course titled "Te Ao Tōrangapū me te Mātauranga/Politics and Philosophy in Education", in the Faculty of Education at The University of Auckland. My primary role was to teach this course to the Māori-medium teacher education students. I was also asked to contribute a lecture in the English-medium programme regarding Māori approaches to politics and philosophy in education. This is a single-semester, 12-week course and I had one lecture space with the English-medium programme to share a kaupapa Māori philosophical stance in education—one lecture in which to discuss moving politics and philosophy beyond the colonial constraints of the academy. Yes, it *is* a big ask and some would argue a tokenistic attempt to include Māori in the course structure.

I committed to doing the lecture for a number of reasons. Confident in my political positioning as a Māori woman in the academy, I want students to know what that means. I want to encourage greater understanding and to contribute to transformative change. I am committed to ensuring that Māori and Pasifika students have their/our stories, content, and philosophies told in the big lecture halls. It is not okay for us to only hear or share our work within the confines of the marae or Māori-medium education. We are in the academy and we are not in here to remain hidden. Moving beyond the colonial constraints of the institution is about taking charge of and building on the opportunities to change the status quo. Being visible is critical to transformative change.

So, in the lecture I discussed kaupapa Māori as a philosophy, as a theory, and as a research methodology. I shared aspects of the mana kaitiakitanga framework and I highlighted the inherently political nature of bringing kaupapa Māori into the academy. I referred to Māori and Indigenous theorists such as those described earlier in this chapter. That was as much as I could do in one lecture. The deeper learning that took the course beyond the university's colonial constraints occurred in tutorial sessions with the Māori-medium programme.

Here, with more time and with total academic control, I was able to reconstruct politics and philosophy within a Māori worldview. Students were tasked with researching the philosophers from their own iwi and hapū. I posed questions that required them to consider the historical development of Māori politics and philosophy. We discussed the politics of resistance to colonial education and the reclamation of our own educational pedagogies and philosophies. In moving forward, this curriculum content needs to be fully explored and developed.

I want to conclude this chapter with an acknowledgment of the great Māori philosophers of Aotearoa. Nei rā te mihi ki a koutou kua huri ki tuā o te ārai. Nei rā te mihi mai i a mātou e hīkoi nei i roto i ā koutou tapuwae. Hei aha? Hei oranga mo ngā tamariki mokopuna, hei oranga whenua hoki. Te Rangi Topeora, Te Whiti o Rongomai, Tohu Kākahi, your legacies, your wisdom and your activism paved the way for us to be as we are today. Upon your work, and that of others who have gone before, the colonial constraints of our academic institutions will be resisted and reclaimed. Tihei Mouri Ora.

## *References*

Bargh, M. (2007). *Resistance: An Indigenous response to neoliberalism.* Wellington: Huia Publishers.

Battiste, M., Bell, L., & Findlay, LM. (2002). Decolonizing education in Canadian universities: An interdisciplinary, international, Indigenous research project. *Canadian Journal of Native Education, 26*(2), 82–95.

Bishop, R. (2008). Te kotahitanga: Kaupapa Māori in mainstream classrooms. In K. Denzin, Y. Lincoln, & L. Tuhiwai Smith (Eds.), *Handbook of critical and Indigenous methodologies* (pp. 497–510). Los Angeles, CA: Sage.

Durie, M. (1998). *Te mana, te kawanatanga: The politics of Māori self-determination.* Auckland: Oxford University Press.

Kidman, J. (2007). *Engaging with Māori communities: An exploration of some tensions in the mediation of social sciences research,* Tihei Oreore Series. Auckland: Ngā Pae o te Māramatanga.

Lee, J. (2009). Decolonising Māori narratives: Pūrakau as method. *Kaupapa Rangahau: A Reader*, 91.

Marsden, M. (1988). The natural world and natural resources: Māori value systems and perspectives. *Resource Management Law Reform No. 29, Part A.* Wellington: Ministry for the Environment.

May, S., & Hill, R. (2005). Māori-medium education: Current issues and challenges. *International Journal of Bilingual Education and Bilingualism, 8*(5), 377–403.

Mead, A.T.P. (1994). *Nga tikanga, nga taonga: Cultural and intellectual property: The rights of indigenous peoples.* Auckland: Te Tara Rangahau o Te Matauranga Māori.

Moorefield, J. (2005). *Te aka: Māori–English dictionary and index.* Auckland: Longman/Pearson Education NZ.

Nepe, T. (1991). *E hao nei e tenei reanga: Te toi huarewa tipuna.* Unpublished master's thesis, The University of Auckland.

Penehira, M. (2011). *Mouri tu, mouri moko, mouri ora! Moko as a wellbeing strategy.* Unpublished doctoral dissertation, The University of Waikato.

Penehira, M., Smith, L. T., Green, A., & Aspin, C. (2011). Mouri matters: Contextualizing mouri in Māori health discourse. *AlterNative: An International Journal of Indigenous Peoples, 7*(2), 177–187.

Pihama, L. (1993). *Tungia te ururua, kia tupu whakaritorito te tupu o te harakeke: A critical analysis of parents as first teachers.* (*RUME Master's Theses Series*, No. 3). Auckland: The University of Auckland.

Pihama, L. (2001). *Tihei mauri ora: Honouring our voices: Mana wahine as kaupapa Māori theoretical framework.* Unpublished doctoral dissertation, The University of Auckland.

Pihama, L. (2005). Asserting indigenous theories of change. In J. Barker (Ed.), *Sovereignty matters: Location of contestation and possibility in indigenous struggles for self-determination* (pp. 191–210). Lincoln, NE: University of Nebraska Press.

Royal, C. (1996, May). *Adventures in mātauranga Māori: Some thoughts on a kawa of Māori knowledge.* Wellington: Victoria University Department of Māori Studies Te Kawa-ā-Māui seminar. Retrieved from http://www.charles-royal.com/

Simons, J. A., & Smith, L. T. (1998). *Ngā kura Māori: The native schools system 1867–1969.* Auckland: Auckland University Press.

Smith, C. W. (2002). *He pou herenga ki te nui: Māori knowledge and the university.* Unpublished doctoral dissertation, The University of Auckland.

Smith, C. W. (2008). In *Tikanga Rangahau* [DVD]. Auckland: Māori and Indigenous Analysis.

Smith, G. H. (1997). *The development of kaupapa Māori: Theory and praxis.* Unpublished doctoral dissertation, The University of Auckland.

Smith, L. T. (1997). *Nga aho o te kakahu matauranga: The multiple layers of struggle by Māori in education.* Unpublished doctoral dissertation, The University of Auckland.

Smith, L. T. (1999). *Decolonising methodologies: Research and indigenous peoples.* London, UK and New York, NY: Zed Books.

Smith, L. T. (2007). Neoliberalism and "endangered authenticities". In M. de la Cadena & O. Starn (Eds.), *Indigenous experience today* (pp. 333–352). Oxford, UK: Berg.

Walker, P. O. (2003). Colonising research: Academia's structural violence towards Indigenous peoples. *Social Alternatives, 22*(3), 37–40.

Walters, K. (2006). Indigenous perspectives in survey research: Conceptualising and measuring historical trauma, microaggressions, and colonial trauma response. In J. Te Rito (Ed.), *Matauranga taketake: Traditional knowledge. Indigenous indicators of well-being: Perspectives, practices, solutions, C*onference proceedings (pp. 27–44). Auckland: Ngā Pae o te Māramatanga.

## Socially critical perspectives
## Discussion starters

1. Socially critical perspectives hold a mirror up to society. What do you see when you hold a mirror up to society? What do we do well? Where do we need to improve?
2. Socially critical perspectives aim to give voice to marginalised groups. Who are the groups most marginalised by society and schooling? What measures need to be taken to redress this?
3. How has the history of Aotearoa New Zealand shaped the education system? How has schooling contributed to pivileging some groups and disadvantaging others?
4. Should social justice be one of the main aims of education? Discuss your views.

# Index

absolutism 71, 73
accountability
    kaupapa Māori researchers 124–25
    teachers 43, 44
achievement disparities 22, 29, 30, 104
affect 54, 55
Apple, Michael 104, 109, 116
arts education 29, 33, 38, 44, 50
Ashton-Warner, Sylvia 38, 51–52
assessment 35, 43, 44, 64, 66
    NCEA 44
    tests 30, 44
associated living 16, 21
Aubert, Mother Suzanne 36
autonomy 10–11, 17–18, 19, 57–58, 68, 71, 74

banking model of education 20, 22
Beeby, Beatrice 39
Beeby, Clarence 28, 29, 37, 38, 50
Bernstein, Basil 82, 88–89
bicultural education 55, 56, 106–07
Bronfenbrenner, Urie 55

charter schools 13, 21, 43
child-centred education *see* student-centred education
children
    circumstances born into 73–75
    "competent, autonomous and flexible" 57–58
    health and welfare 37
    indigenous Māori image 55–56
    liberal commitment to 68, 79
    nature of 35
choice 43, 48, 78, 98, 100, 115
    reasoned and informed 17–18
Christchurch Open-Air League 37
citizenship 18, 29, 49, 57, 68
colonisation 99
    *see also* decolonisation
    and kaupapa Māori 121–27
    moving beyond colonial constraints 131–32
"coming to know" 11
community empowerment 107
competencies 14, 83
    measurable 11
competition 51, 72
conceptual progression 76, 77
constructivism 55, 57
co-operation 42, 53
creativity 32, 35, 44, 48
crèches 36
critical literacy 100
critical theory 98–99, 100, 104
    characteristics 106–08
    description 105
    and education 110–12, 113, 114–16
    origins 104–05
curriculum 13, 17–19, 22, 34, 36, 39, 43, 48, 83
    cross-curricular connections 40, 41, 43, 44
    disciplinary knowledge 86, 88
    distinction between curriculum and pedagogy 84–85
    emergent 56, 57
    knowledge-centred 92
    NCEA 44
    *New Zealand Curriculum* (Ministry of Education, 2007) 12, 23–24, 42

normative 57–58
purpose: the intellectual development of students 85
re-imagining 55
social construction 56–57
Steiner 33
Te Whāriki (Ministry of Education, 1996) 42–43, 47–48, 49, 50, 55–58
Currie Commission 40

Dean, M. 2–3
decile system 113–15
decolonisation 120, 122, 125, 126, 127
see also colonisation
democracy 19, 20, 30, 71, 73, 78
  education as preparation for democratic living 16–17, 21, 34, 51
  participatory 16, 20, 21, 23–24, 107, 108–09, 110
  personal freedom 18, 71, 73
Depression, 1930s 28, 37, 50
Dewey, John 16–17, 21, 28, 33–34, 45, 48, 49, 51–55
  *Experience and Education* (1938) 86, 91
  *Froebel's Educational Principles* (1915) 53
disciplinary learning and knowledge 18–19, 30, 75, 84, 85–87, 88, 92
diversity 16, 51, 54, 108, 110

early childhood education 44
  see also kindergartens; Playcentre movement
  for-profit centres 44

post-foundational perspectives 52, 54
progressive tradition 48–52
Reconceptualising Early Childhood 49
Te Whāriki (Ministry of Education, 1996) 42–43, 47–48, 49, 50, 55–58
education
  see also early childhood education; liberal education; progressive education
  banking model 20, 22
  enduring questions 12–15, 24
  holistic 32–33, 37, 40, 44, 48, 56, 100, 104
  as ideas 10, 11, 12–13, 25
  moral and ethical aspects 11–12, 17–19, 23, 34, 45
  nebulous nature 11
  normative claims 14–15
  pragmatic 49, 51, 54, 57
  as preparation for democratic living 16–17, 21, 34, 51
  problem-posing 20, 34, 44, 53
  purposes and aims 13, 14, 16–17, 23, 35, 43, 57, 68
  role of the state 13
  as a state of mind 18–19
  student-centred 29, 34, 41–42, 43, 44, 48, 50, 55, 69, 83, 91, 92
Education Act 1877 36, 50
elitism 36, 44, 71, 75, 77, 78
emancipation 51, 75, 76, 97, 99, 100, 106, 107–08
emergence of meaning 56–57, 58, 87, 92
empowerment 42, 57, 66, 76, 78, 100, 106, 107

Enlightenment (European intellectual movement) 68, 69, 76
enlightenment (process of "raising the consciousness") 107
equal opportunity 68, 69, 75, 110
equality and inequality 30, 70, 71–72, 75, 78, 79, 121
    privilege and disadvantage in Aotearoa New Zealand 28, 51, 99, 104, 112–16
equity and inequity 22, 23, 68, 69, 72, 104, 108, 110, 111, 113, 115–16
evaluation by teachers 90
experience-based learning 17, 18, 21, 34, 44, 48, 49, 50, 51, 52–53, 86

Fendalton School, Christchurch 37
foundational knowledge 76–77
Frankfurt School 104–05
Fraser, Nancy 108–09, 110
Fraser, Peter 28–29, 37, 38, 69
freedom
    *see also* liberty
    individual 18, 67, 68, 69, 70, 72, 76
    in thinking and learning 51, 53, 54, 70
free-market policies 43–44, 51, 56, 72, 113
Freire, Paulo 19–20, 22, 74, 100
Froebel, Friedrich 32–33, 36, 50, 51, 53
fundamental knowledge 76–77, 78

generalisability of knowledge 76–77

Habens, William 50
Hall, Granville Stanley 53

hau 127
hau āio (breath of life) 130
hau moana (breath of sea) 131
hau ora (holistic health) 130, 131
hau tangata (breath of humanity) 131
hau whenua (breath of land) 130–31
hēlhara (wrong) 129
Hobbes, Thomas 71, 72
Hogben, George 36
Hohepa, Margie 98
holistic education 32–33, 37, 40, 44, 48, 56, 100, 104
human rights 70, 71, 110

ideas
    education as ideas 10, 11, 12–13, 24
    teachers' engagement with ideas 10, 11
inclusivity 104
income inequality in Aotearoa New Zealand 112–16
Indigenous peoples 119–20, 121–22, 125
Indigenous Research Agenda 125–26
individualism 43, 51, 91
    socially responsible 16–17
industrial models of education 49, 50
inequality *see* equality and inequality
inequity *see* equity and inequity
initial teacher education
    *see also* preservice teachers
    philosophical questioning and thinking 10, 11, 12, 13, 15, 21–24
    shifting from universities into schools 22
insider–outsider research 124
institutional constraints on social justice 109, 111

intellectual capital  19
intrinsic motivation and value  77–78
Isaacs, Susan  39

Jefferson, Thomas  73, 74, 78
Jenkins, Kuni  98
Joyce, Stephen  77

Kant, Immanuel  68, 76, 79
karakia (prayer or incantation)  129–30
kaupapa Māori theory and research  98, 99–100, 119–20, 132
   and colonisation  121–27
   mana kaitiakitanga framework  127–31, 132
kindergartens  33, 36, 50, 51
knowledge  13, 83, 84
   best knowledge to teach  17–19
   disciplinary learning and knowledge  18–19, 30, 75, 84, 85–87, 88, 92
   dispositions required for encountering  11
   everyday knowledge  84, 85–87, 88, 90
   fundamentality and generality  76–77, 78
   powerful knowledge  68, 69, 75, 84, 87–88, 92
   role in freedom and liberty  70
   social construction  105
   transformative power  63–66
   value of  15
knowledge equivalence  88

Labour governments  28–29, 37, 40
learner-centred schools  17
learnification  84, 88
learning
   *see also* experience-based learning; freedom – in thinking and learning
   activities  35
   beliefs about  35
   setting  35
   social context  53–54
liberal education  17–19, 22–23, 44, 48, 50, 63–66, 68–69, 73–79, 83
   characteristics  75–78
   principles  68
liberalism  70
   *see also* neoliberalism
   classical  71
   social  71–72
liberty  70, 71–72, 73–75, 76, 78
   *see also* freedom
literacy  20, 22, 44
   critical  100
Locke, John  32, 50
   *Two Treatises of Government* (1772/2002)  71

mana kaitiakitanga framework  127–31, 132
Māori
   *see also* bicultural education; kaupapa Māori theory and research
   assimilation policies  49, 121
   culture and language in *Te Whāriki*  42, 55–56
   principle of wellbeing  127–31
   rights and emancipation  51
   self-determination  99, 123
   students, priority learner group  104
   Sylvia Ashton-Warner's teaching  38
   traditional systems of learning  36, 49, 55–56

tribal nature of communities 124–25
market forces 43–44, 51, 56, 72, 113
Marsden, Samuel 127
Marx, Karl 19, 104
Master of Teaching programme 22
Mill, John Stuart 74
mind–body dualism 48, 54
Ministry of Education 12, 22, 104
missionary-led education 49
mixed modality approach 88–91
Montessori, Maria 33
Montessori preschools 36
mouri 127, 128, 131
mouri ora (life force) 130

National Certificate of Education (NCEA) 44
National Standards 13, 22–23, 43, 44
Native Schools Act 1847 49
Neill, A. S. 34
neoconservatism 43, 44
neoliberalism 29–30, 43–44, 48, 51, 57, 72–73, 113
Nepe, Tuakana 124–25
*Neue Schule* (New School) movement 34
New Education Fellowship (NEF) 28, 37, 39
    conference in New Zealand, 1937 37–38, 50
"new maths" 40
"new social studies" 40
New Zealand Constitution Act 1853 73
*New Zealand Curriculum* (Ministry of Education, 2007) 12, 23–24, 42
*noa* (normal) 129
normative claims in education 14–15

Nuffield Science Project 40
numeracy 22, 44

open-air classrooms 37
Oruaiti School, Northland 38

pacing of learning 90
Paraha, Glenys 98
parity of esteem 88
participatory democracy 16, 20, 21, 23–24, 107, 108–09, 110
Pasifika students, priority learner group 104
pedagogy 57, 83
    distinction between curriculum and pedagogy 84–85
    everyday knowledge as a resource 86, 88, 90
    Freire 19–20
    influence of progressive education 31, 34, 44–45, 48, 50
    mixed modality approach 88–91
    as a relationship 52, 54, 58
personal philosophies of teaching 1, 15, 23–24
Pestalozzi, Johann 32, 33
Peters, R. S. 18–19
philosophical thinking 10, 11–12, 13, 24
    on educational issues 21–24
    questions 12–15, 24
Piaget, Jean 55
Pihama, Leonie 98, 99
PISA (Programme for International Student Assessment) 22
play 29, 33, 36, 37, 39, 44, 51, 53–54
Playcentre movement 38–39
"playway" methods 39
Plunket Society 37

policy
- contextual underpinnings 12
- teachers as mediators between policy and practice 11

politics 106–07, 109, 111
- macropolitics and education 112–14
- mesopolitics and education 114–15
- micropolitics and education 115–16

*pono* (truth) 129
post-foundational perspectives 52, 54
poverty 112–13
power relations 98, 99, 100, 105, 106, 116
- in education 19, 20, 100

powerful knowledge 68, 69, 75, 84, 87–88, 92
practice 1, 22, 48
- contextual underpinnings 12
- mixed modality approach 88–91
- strengthening 11
- teachers as mediators between policy and practice 11

pragmatic education 49, 51, 54, 57
praxis 20, 56
preservice teachers 1, 13
- *see also* initial teacher education
- demand for practical learning 10

privatisation 51
problem-posing education 20, 34, 44, 53
progressive education 27–30, 31, 83
- characteristics 35
- critiques 39–40
- development in New Zealand 36–39, 49–50
- in early childhood 48–52
- early development of 32–34
- limitations 83–84, 91–92
- ongoing transformation through reflection 54
- reflections on being a progressive teacher 40–42
- re-imagining 55, 58
- today 42–45

progressive politics 28

questioning 98–99
- in education 12–15, 24

rational thinking and knowledge 52, 68, 69, 70, 73
Rawls, John 108
reason, development of 78
reconceptualist movement 49, 52
Richardson, Elwyn 29, 38, 51–52
Rousseau, Jean-Jacques 36, 50
- *Emile, or On Education* (1762) 32

Samoan woman in Aotearoa New Zealand, voice and choice 98, 99, 100
school zoning 113, 114
science education 40, 50
selection of content for teaching 89
self-determination 68, 69, 109, 110
- Indigenous peoples 126
- Māori 99, 123

self-managing schools 44
sequence of concepts, teaching 89–90
Shelley, James 37
Sisters of Compassion 36
Smith, Linda Tuhiwai 120, 122, 125–26
social contract 71

social justice  20, 30, 37, 51, 68, 72, 75, 98, 99, 105, 108
  definition  108–09
  in education  29, 110, 115
socialisation  10–11, 68
special education needs  104
state
  intervention  72
  role in education  13
Steiner, Rudolf  33
Stephenson, Maxine  98
student-centred education  29, 34, 41–42, 43, 44, 48, 50, 55, 69, 83, 91, 92
student–teacher mode of interaction  90–91
student–teacher power relationships  19, 20, 22
subjectivity in research  123–24
Summerhill  34, 40

Tamariki School, Christchurch  40
tangata whenua (people of the land)  131
*tapu* (sacred)  129
Te Ao Māori worldview  48
*Te Whāriki* (Ministry of Education, 1996)  42–43, 47–48, 49, 50, 55–58
Te Whiti o Rongomai  133
Teach First NZ  22
teachers
  *see also* pedagogy; practice; preservice teachers
  accountability  43, 44
  as critical practitioners  11, 14, 23
  engagement with ideas  10, 11, 24
  as ethical and political agents  19–20, 23, 34
  mediators between policy and practice  11
  mode of interaction with students  90–91
  personal philosophies of teaching  1, 15, 23–24
  power relationships with students  19, 20, 22
  professional identities  11, 14, 21, 23
  qualities  20
  role in progressive education  35
Thomas Report, 1944  39
thought collectives  2–3, 4
tika (correct)  129
tikanga Māori  127, 128
Tohu Kākahi  133
*Tomorrow's Schools* (Lange, 1988)  29–30, 44
Topeora, Te Rangi  133
Tovey, Gordon  29
tuakana–teina relationship  124–25
tyranny of tradition  71, 73

voice  98–101
Vygotsky, Lev  55, 86, 87, 90, 92

Waikerepuru, Huirangi  127, 130
wairua (spirituality)  130
Waldorf schools  33
wealth inequality in Aotearoa New Zealand  112–16
Wilson, Arnold Manaaki  29
Wollstonecraft, Mary, *A Vindication of the Rights of Woman* (1792)  32, 70, 73
women's activism  51

Young, Iris Marion  106, 109

zoning for schools  113, 114

www.ingramcontent.com/pod-product-compliance
Lightning Source LLC
Chambersburg PA
CBHW080636230426
43663CB00016B/2891